Decades of the 20th Century
Dekaden des 20. Jahrhunderts
Décennies du XXe siècle

Nick Yapp

KÖNEMANN

This edition ©KÖNEMANN*, an imprint of Tandem Verlag GmbH, Königswinter
Photographs ©2001 Getty Images

This book was produced by Getty Images
Unique House, 21–31 Woodfield Road, London W9 2BA

For KÖNEMANN*:	For Getty Images:
Managing editor: Sally Bald	Art director: Michael Rand
Project editors: Lucile Bas, Meike Hilbring	Design: Tea McAleer
Translation into German: Christian Rochow	Picture editor: Ali Khoja
Translation into French: Francine Rey	Editor: Richard Collins
	Proof reader: Liz Ihre

*KÖNEMANN is a registered trademark of Tandem Verlag GmbH

Printed in Germany

ISBN 3-8331-1084-8

10 9 8 7 6 5 4 3 2 1
X IX VIII VII VI V IV III II I

Frontispiece: The spirit of the age. A Salvadorean soldier runs for cover
during an exchange of gunfire with FMLN guerrillas in the city of Apopa.
Civil war raged across El Salvador throughout the 1980s.

Frontispiz: Der Geist des Zeitalters. Ein salvadorianischer Soldat sucht
Deckung während eines Feuergefechts mit FMLN-Guerilleros in der Stadt
Apopa. In den achtziger Jahren tobte ein Bürgerkrieg in El Salvador.

Frontispice : L'air du temps. Un soldat salvadorien court se mettre à l'abri
durant un échange de coups de feu avec les membres de la guerrilla FMLN
dans la ville d'Apopa. La guerre civile fit rage dans tout le Salvador durant
les années 1980.

Contents / Inhalt / Sommaire

Introduction

True to the formula recommended for modern movie plots, the 20th century reached crisis point as it approached its end. The tension between haves and have-nots, between power and the people, between labour and capital increased dramatically. The old tools of negotiation and compromise seemed inadequate for the job in hand – driving the world forward to new economies, new alliances, new social structures. Unemployment became a condition rather than a temporary misfortune for millions. Democracy became the servant rather than the basis of government. The lack of personal freedom under Communism became overwhelmingly more important than the security the system offered.

The result was a series of explosions – some of mighty proportions. There were wars of old-fashioned colonial-style simplicity (in the Falklands, Grenada, Libya, Zimbabwe) and of new complexity (in the Lebanon, Afghanistan, Angola). An epidemic of riots and revolutions brought down governments in Haiti, Poland, El Salvador, the Philippines and Panama; and tested the mettle of others in India, Chile, Britain, South Africa, France and South Korea. Most of the satellite governments of Eastern Europe managed to maintain their trembling hold on a withering authority into the 1990s.

There were new kids on the block, new faces in new places. The yuppie emerged as the Bright Young Thing of the Eighties – proud, ambitious, hard working but myopic. New Man washed up, fed his babies, cleaned the house and battled to erase (or at least limit) the worst side effects of his testosterone. Women invaded what had formerly been 'men only' arenas. In September 1983 the United States selected its first black Miss America.

And the world continued to crash its gears, never certain whether it wished to go forward or backwards. The last Playboy club closed in 1988. Texas voted to cease teaching the theory of evolution in 1984. Capital punishment returned to many American states. The first female astronauts came on stream. The Jeep made a comeback. The stealth bomber made its sinister debut. A solar-powered aircraft flew the Channel. A baboon's heart was implanted in a baby. The world stock markets soared in August 1987 and crashed two months later.

There were gluts of oil and desperate shortages of food. The worst drought for fifty years parched much of the world's surface in 1988. Pollution established itself as a major player on the world scene, with the horrors of Chernobyl and Bhopal well to the fore. The worst ever air disaster occurred on Mount Osutaka, Japan, in August 1985. An earthquake devastated Armenia in December 1988.

Through it all shone the hope and enthusiasm of the human race – ever-ingenious, ever-inventive, ever-industrious… but perhaps for a brief moment losing some of its concern for its fellows and its planet.

Einleitung

Getreu dem bewährten Rezept moderner Unterhaltungsfilme lief das 20. Jahrhundert gegen Ende auf einen Spannungshöhepunkt zu. Die Gegensätze zwischen Reich und Arm, zwischen Machthabern und Volk, zwischen Arbeit und Kapital verschärften sich dramatisch. Die alten Mittel von Verhandlungen und Ausgleich schienen ungeeignet für die anstehenden Aufgaben – die Schaffung neuer Ökonomien, neuer Bündnisse und neuer sozialer Strukturen. Die Arbeitslosigkeit wurde für Millionen von einem zeitlich begrenzten Unglück zu einem Dauerzustand. Die Demokratie wurde zum Dienstboten, statt zur Grundlage der Regierenden. Für die Menschen, die in kommunistischen Systemen lebten, wurde die fehlende Freiheit wichtiger als die vom System garantierte Sicherheit.

Das Ergebnis waren eine Reihe zum Teil gewaltiger Umbrüche. Es gab Kriege nach dem altbekannten einfachen Muster der Kolonialzeit (auf den Falklandinseln, auf Grenada, in Libyen und Simbabwe) und Kriege von neuer Komplexität (im Libanon, in Afghanistan und Angola). Eine Epidemie von Aufständen und Revolutionen führte zum Sturz der Regierungen Haitis, Polens, El Salvadors, der Philippinen und Panamas, während sich die Regierungen Indiens, Chiles, Großbritanniens, Südafrikas, Frankreichs und Südkoreas gegen ähnliche Schwierigkeiten behaupten konnten. Den Herrschenden der meisten osteuropäischen Satellitenstaaten gelang es, ihre schwindende Macht noch bis in die neunziger Jahre hinein zu behalten.

Eine neue Jugend war da, an neuen Orten sah man neue Gesichter. Der Yuppie – stolz, ehrgeizig und hart arbeitend, dabei aber kurzsichtig – gab in den achtziger Jahren seinen Einstand. Der „neue Mann" erledigte den Abwasch, fütterte das Baby, putzte die Wohnung und mühte sich, die schlimmsten Nebenwirkungen seines Testosterons zu beseitigen (oder sie wenigstens irgendwie in den Griff zu bekommen). Die Frauen drangen in Bereiche vor, die bislang den Männern vorbehalten waren. Im September 1983 wurde in den USA erstmals eine Afroamerikanerin zur Miss America gewählt.

Und allseits ging es in hohem Tempo weiter, nur war nie klar, ob es sich bei den Neuerungen um Fort- oder Rückschritte handelte. Der letzte Playboy-Club schloss 1988. In Texas bestimmten die Wähler 1984, dass die Evolutionstheorie nicht mehr in den Schulen gelehrt werden dürfe. In vielen US-Bundesstaaten wurde die Hinrichtung wieder eingeführt. Es gab die ersten weiblichen Astronauten. Der Jeep erlebte ein Comeback. Der Tarnkappenbomber feierte sein unheimliches Debüt. Ein Flugzeug, das von Solarenergie gespeist wurde, überquerte den Ärmelkanal. Einem Baby wurde ein Pavianherz eingepflanzt. Die Aktienmärkte setzten im August 1987 zu einem Höhenflug an und brachen zwei Monate später zusammen.

Der Markt wurde mit Öl überschwemmt, aber gleichzeitig gab es furchtbare Hungersnöte. Die schlimmste Dürre seit 50 Jahren suchte 1988 einen großen Teil des Erdballs heim. Die Umweltverschmutzung wurde zu einem wichtigen Thema, die Katastrophen von Tschernobyl und Bhopal erregten weltweites Entsetzen. Der schlimmste Flugzeugabsturz aller Zeiten ereignete sich im August 1985 auf dem japanischen Berg Osutaka. Armenien wurde im Dezember 1988 von einem Erdbeben verwüstet.

Durch all diese Ereignisse hindurch blieben die Hoffnungen und die Begeisterungsfähigkeit der Menschheit, ihre Erfindungskraft, ihr Einfallsreichtum und ihr Fleiß sichtbar – doch manchmal auch ihre Sorglosigkeit im Umgang mit dem Mitmenschen und dem Planeten.

Introduction

Conformément à la formule recommandée dans les scénarios du cinéma moderne, le XXᵉ siècle atteignit un point critique alors qu'il touchait à sa fin. La tension entre les nantis et les pauvres, entre le pouvoir et le peuple, entre le travail et le capital, augmentait dangereusement. Les outils autrefois utilisés pour négocier et parvenir à des compromis semblaient inadéquats pour accomplir les tâches qui s'imposaient, comme celle de conduire le monde vers de nouvelles économies, de nouvelles alliances et de nouvelles structures sociales. Pour des millions de malheureux, le chômage devint un statut et non plus une situation temporaire. La démocratie se mit au service des gouvernements plutôt que l'inverse. Le manque de liberté individuelle sous le régime communiste fut contesté en masse, devenant plus vital que la sécurité garantie par le système.

Il en résulta une série d'explosions dont certaines furent bouleversantes. Il y eut des guerres coloniales, menées avec des méthodes éprouvées et simplistes – dans les Falkland, à Grenade, en Libye, au Zimbabwe – et d'autres guerres qui révélèrent une complexité nouvelle – au Liban, en Afghanistan, en Angola. Une épidémie d'émeutes et de révolutions fit tomber les gouvernements de Haïti, de Pologne, du Salvador, des Philippines et du Panama tandis qu'elle mit à l'épreuve d'autres pouvoirs, en Inde, au Chili, en Grande-Bretagne, en Afrique du Sud, en France et en Corée du Sud. En dépit d'une autorité déclinante, les pays satellites de l'Europe de l'Est surent contenir les masses grondantes jusqu'à l'aube des années quatre-vingt-dix.

Une génération nouvelle émergea, avec de nouvelles têtes à de nouveaux postes. Le yuppie devint le petit génie des années quatre-vingt, fier, ambitieux, travailleur mais myope. L'homme nouveau faisait la vaisselle, s'occupait des gosses, faisait le ménage et s'employait à effacer (ou du moins limiter) les effets secondaires et désagréables du machisme. Les femmes, quant à elles, envahirent les territoires jusque-là réservés aux hommes. En septembre 1983, les États-Unis élirent pour la première fois une Noire au titre de Miss Amérique.

Pendant ce temps, le monde continuait à appuyer sur l'accélérateur, sans jamais trop savoir s'il fallait avancer ou reculer. Le dernier club Play Boy ferma ses portes en 1988. L'État du Texas vota le retrait de l'enseignement de la théorie de l'évolution en 1984. La peine de mort fut à nouveau appliquée dans de nombreux États américains. Les premières femmes astronautes furent enrôlées. La Jeep marqua son grand retour. Le bombardier invisible fit ses sinistres débuts tandis qu'un avion à énergie solaire réussissait à voler au-dessus de la Manche. Un cœur de babouin fut implanté sur un bébé. Les marchés boursiers du monde entier montèrent en flèche en août 1987 avant de s'effondrer deux mois plus tard.

Il y avait des surplus de pétrole et des manques de nourriture désespérants. En 1988, une grande partie de la planète fut ravagée par la sécheresse, la plus grave de ces 50 dernières années. La pollution commençait à jouer un rôle majeur partout dans le monde, Tchernobyl et Bhopal en furent les illustrations les plus horribles. La plus grave catastrophe aérienne survint au Mont Osutaka au Japon en août 1985 et un tremblement de terre dévasta l'Arménie en 1988.

Cette décennie fut marquée par l'espoir et l'enthousiasme d'une race humaine qui semblait toujours plus intelligente, plus inventive, plus travailleuse … mais cette dernière oublia temporairement de se soucier de ses semblables et de la planète.

1. Movers and shakers
Menschen, die Geschichte machten
Progressistes et agitateurs

Heading for re-election. A Churchillian portrait of Margaret Thatcher, March 1983. Two months later the Iron Lady won a second term in office and intensified her campaign to change the face of Britain.

Auf dem Weg zur Wiederwahl. Margaret Thatcher in Churchill-Pose, März 1983. Zwei Monate später wurde die „Eiserne Lady" wiedergewählt und setzte ihre Politik zur durchgreifenden Umgestaltung Großbritanniens verstärkt fort.

Sur le chemin d'une réélection. Portrait de Margaret Thatcher aux allures churchilliennes, mars 1983. Élue deux mois plus tard pour un second mandat, la Dame de fer intensifia son action pour changer le visage de la Grande-Bretagne.

1. Movers and shakers
Menschen, die Geschichte machten
Progressistes et agitateurs

An almost totally new cast was assembled for the dramas of the 1980s. Thatcher and the Ayatollah Khomeini had both come to power in 1979, but Reagan and Bush, Mugabe, Jaruzelski and Walesa, Gorbachev, Mitterrand and Kohl were all new on the scene. Together, they and dozens of others presided over a decade that saw the end of the world that had been constructed after the Second World War, and the beginning of political post-modernism.

They set about their appointed tasks with single-minded gusto that polarised the political scene. What they had to offer were new solutions directed at new problems – global communication, market economies, managing nuclear waste – rather than the eternal problems of poverty, disease, famine and oppression.

They shook much of the world by the scruff of its neck, administering the last rites to traditional trade unionism, to one-nation conservatism, to the Berlin Wall. They initiated the later collapse of the Soviet Empire. When, however, the dust settled a decade or so later, the world was recognisably the same – warts and all.

Die politische Bühne der achtziger Jahre zeigte eine fast völlig neue Besetzung. Thatcher und der Ayatollah Khomeini waren bereits 1979 an die Macht gekommen, nun kamen Reagan und Bush, Mugabe, Jaruzelski und Walesa, Gorbatschow, Mitterrand und Kohl neu hinzu. Diese Politiker und viele weitere regierten in einem Jahrzehnt, in dem die nach dem Zweiten Weltkrieg etablierte Weltordnung zu Ende ging und die politische Postmoderne anbrach.

Die Regierenden gingen teilweise mit einer Entschlossenheit an ihre Aufgaben, die zu einer Polarisierung der politischen Haltungen führte. Sie stellten sich neuen Problemen, für die sie neue Lösungen suchten – die weltweite Kommunikation, die Ausweitung der Marktwirtschaft, die Bewältigung des Atommülls –, und weniger den ewigen Fragestellungen wie Armut, Krankheit, Hunger und Unterdrückung.

Sie packten althergebrachte Gewohnheiten beim Kragen, erteilten der traditionellen Gewerkschaftsmacht, dem nationalen Konservativismus und der Berliner Mauer die letzte Ölung. Sie leiteten den späteren Zusammenbruch der Sowjetunion ein. Als sich dann aber nach wieder einem Jahrzehnt der Staub gelegt hatte, war die Welt erkennbar die gleiche – mit all ihren Schwächen.

Pour affronter les événements des années quatre-vingt, il y eut un renouvellement presque complet des acteurs de la scène politique. Thatcher et l'ayatollah Khomeiny accédèrent au pouvoir en 1979 déjà tandis que Reagan et Bush, Mugabe, Jaruzelski et Walesa, Gorbatchev, Mitterrand et Kohl n'allaient pas tarder à entrer en scène pour la première fois. Ensemble, avec une douzaine d'autres dirigeants, ils furent aux commandes de cette décennie qui vécut la fin du monde tel qu'il avait été créé après la Seconde Guerre mondiale pour entrer dans l'ère du post-modernisme politique.

Ces hommes d'État se mirent à l'œuvre avec enthousiasme et détermination, ce qui partagea la scène politique en deux pôles. Ils durent imaginer de nouvelles solutions pour de nouveaux problèmes (la communication à l'échelle mondiale, les économies de marché, la gestion des déchets nucléaires) en lieu et place des problèmes qui existaient depuis toujours (la pauvreté, les maladies, la faim et l'oppression des masses).

Ils secouèrent le monde, du moins une grande partie, par la peau du cou, dispensant les derniers rites du syndicalisme traditionnel, du conservatisme de « la » nation, du mur de Berlin. Ils mirent en route le processus qui allait mettre fin à l'Empire soviétique. Il n'empêche qu'une dizaine d'années plus tard, quand le calme se fit à nouveau, il fallut constater que le monde n'avait pratiquement pas changé et qu'il n'y avait guère d'amélioration à signaler.

Mikhail Gorbachev of the Soviet Union (left) and Ronald Reagan of the United States meet beneath their respective flags at the Geneva Summit, 19 November 1985. Little was achieved beyond reducing international tension.

Der sowjetische Parteichef Michail Gorbatschow (links) und der amerikanische Präsident Ronald Reagan unter den Flaggen ihrer Staaten beim Gipfeltreffen in Genf am 19. November 1985, bei dem, abgesehen von einer gewissen Abnahme der internationalen Spannungen, wenig erreicht wurde.

Mikhail Gorbatchev de l'Union soviétique (à gauche) et Ronald Reagan des États-Unis se rencontrent sous leurs drapeaux respectifs au sommet de Genève, le 19 novembre 1985. Cette rencontre n'aboutit à aucun résultat concret, mais permit de diminuer la tension internationale.

WHITE HOUSE/BLACK STAR/COLORIFIC!

(Opposite) The balloonatic. Ronald Reagan peeps through a sea of balloons in Iowa during his 1984 presidential campaign. (Above) Not her usual dummy. Nancy Reagan (right), the First Lady, clowns her way through cabaret time at the annual Congressional barbecue held in the Diplomatic Reception Room of the White House, Washington, DC.

(Gegenüberliegende Seite) Kaum noch Durchblick. Ronald Reagan inmitten eines Luftballonmeers bei einem Wahl-kampfauftritt in Iowa, 1984. (Oben) Mal nicht an der Seite des üblichen Partners. First Lady Nancy Reagan (rechts) versucht sich während des alljährlichen Kongress-Barbecues im Empfangssaal des Weißen Hauses in Washington, D. C., als Clown.

(Ci-contre) Simplet parmi les ballons. En campagne présidentielle dans l'Iowa, Ronald Reagan émerge d'une mer de ballons, 1984. (Ci-dessus) Encore plus clownesque que d'habitude. Nancy Reagan (à droite), première dame des États-Unis, donne la répartie au clown du spectacle du traditionnel barbecue annuel du Congrès organisé dans la Salle de réception des diplomates de la Maison Blanche à Washington.

HULTON|ARCHIVE

(Opposite) Step aside Blue Eyes. Reagan cuts in on Frank Sinatra to dance with his wife Nancy in the White House East Room, 9 February 1981. (Above) Reagan with President-elect George Bush (right), 20 January 1989.

(Gegenüberliegende Seite) Na, das wird ein bisschen eng. Reagan greift ein, als Ehefrau Nancy im Ostsaal des Weißen Hauses ein Tänzchen mit Frank Sinatra wagt, 9. Februar 1981. (Oben) Reagan mit seinem gewählten Nachfolger George Bush (rechts) am 20. Januar 1989.

(Ci-contre) Dégage Frankie. Reagan s'interpose auprès de Frank Sinatra pour exiger une danse de sa femme dans la salle de bal de la Maison Blanche, le 9 février 1981. (Ci-dessus) Reagan en compagnie du président élu, George Bush (à droite), le 20 janvier 1989.

RICK FRIEDMAN/BLACK STAR/COLORIFIC!

(Above and opposite) Moment of relief. George Bush and his wife Barbara at the Republican Party National Convention, New Orleans, 18 August 1988. In 1980 Bush had contested the Republican presidential nomination with Reagan.

(Oben und gegenüberliegende Seite) Ein Augenblick der Erleichterung. George Bush und Ehefrau Barbara beim Wahlparteitag der Republikaner in New Orleans, 18. August 1988. 1980 war Bush bei der Nominierung des Präsidentschaftskandidaten gegen Reagan angetreten.

(Ci-dessus et ci-contre) Moment de soulagement. George Bush et sa femme Barbara à la Convention nationale du Parti républicain, Nouvelle-Orléans, 18 août 1988. En 1980, Bush avait disputé le ticket républicain pour l'élection présidentielle aux côtés de Reagan.

For the next eight years he was the best of Vice-Presidents, loyal and uncharismatic, playing an important role in forming and implementing foreign policy, and successfully skating over the thin ice of Irangate.

In den folgenden acht Jahren war er ein hervorragender Vizepräsident, loyal und unauffällig, der eine wichtige Rolle bei der Gestaltung und Umsetzung der amerikanischen Außenpolitik spielte und sich sicher über das dünne Eis der Iran-Contra-Affäre bewegte.

Il fut, pendant les huit années qui suivirent, le meilleur des vice-présidents, à la fois loyal et charismatique tout en jouant un rôle important dans la préparation et la mise en œuvre de la politique étrangère. Il esquiva le scandale de l'Irangate avec brio.

KEYSTONE/HULTON|ARCHIVE

Bad days at Brighton. (Above) At the 1985 Tory Party Conference, Margaret Thatcher is perhaps haunted by memories of the previous year's bombing. (Opposite) Neil Kinnock's sad imitation of King Canute, 2 October 1983.

Schwere Tage in Brighton. (Oben) Auf dem Parteitag der Konservativen (1985) wird Margaret Thatcher möglicherweise von Erinnerungen an den Bombenanschlag im Vorjahr heimgesucht. (Gegenüberliegende Seite) So wird das nichts. Schnappschuss des britischen Oppositionsführers Neil Kinnock, 2. Oktober 1983.

Mauvais temps à Brighton. (Ci-dessus) Margaret Thatcher, lors de la conférence du parti conservateur en 1985, serait-elle hantée par le souvenir de l'attentat à la bombe perpétré l'année précédente ? (Ci-contre) Neil Kinnock imite bien mal le roi Canut, 2 octobre 1983.

Underground power. Chancellor Helmut Kohl of West Germany emerges from a visit to the coalface of a mine.

Der schwarze Riese. Bundeskanzler Helmut Kohl nach dem Besuch einer Steinkohlenzeche.

Pouvoir souterrain. Helmut Kohl, chancelier de l'Allemagne de l'Ouest, émerge d'une visite sur le front de taille d'une mine.

Underwater deterrent.
President François
Mitterrand attends
the inauguration of
the French nuclear
submarine *Inflexible*,
Brest, 1985.

Abschreckung von
unten. Präsident
François Mitterrand
wohnt dem Stapel-
lauf des französischen
Atomunterseeboots
Inflexible bei,
Brest, 1985.

Pouvoir sous-marin.
Le président François
Mitterrand participe
à l'inauguration d'un
sous-marin nucléaire
français, l'*Inflexible*,
à Brest en 1985.

WHITE HOUSE/HULTON | ARCHIVE

'Honey, I forgot to duck.' The immediate aftermath of John Hinckley Jnr's assassination attempt on President Reagan, outside the Washington Hilton Hotel, 30 March 1981. Reagan was wounded in the left lung.

„Schatz, ich hätte mich ducken sollen." Das Foto enstand wenige Sekunden, nachdem John Hinckley jr. vor dem Washingtoner Hilton-Hotel am 30. März 1981 auf Ronald Reagan geschossen hatte. Der Präsident wurde dabei an der linken Lunge verletzt.

« Chérie, j'ai oublié de me baisser. » Cliché pris sitôt après la tentative d'assassinat du président Reagan par John Hinckley Junior devant l'hôtel Hilton de Washington, le 30 mars 1981. Reagan fut blessé au poumon gauche.

Pope John Paul II is lifted from his 'popemobile' after being shot in the stomach by Mehmet Ali Agca, St Peter's Square, Rome, 13 May 1981. Eighteen months later, the Pope visited Ali Agca in gaol to offer his forgiveness.

Papst Johannes Paul II. wird aus seinem „Papamobil" gehoben, kurz nachdem ihm Mehmet Ali Agca in den Bauch geschossen hat, Petersplatz, Rom, 13. Mai 1981. 18 Monate später besuchte der Papst den Attentäter im Gefängnis und vergab ihm.

Le pape Jean Paul II est extrait de son « papamobile » après avoir reçu une balle dans l'estomac tirée par Mehmet Ali Agca, sur la place Saint-Pierre, Rome, le 13 mai 1981. Dix-huit mois plus tard, le pape rendit visite à Ali Agca en prison pour lui donner son pardon.

President Anwar Sadat of Egypt, 13 February 1981. Three years earlier, he and Menachem Begin of Israel had jointly received the Nobel Peace Prize.

Der ägyptische Präsident Anwar al-Sadat, 13. Februar 1981. Drei Jahre zuvor hatten er und der israelische Ministerpräsident Menachem Begin den Friedensnobelpreis erhalten.

Le président égyptien Anouar al-Sadate, 13 février 1981. Trois ans plus tôt, lui et Menahem Begin d'Israël avaient reçu ensemble le prix Nobel de la paix.

NAKRAM AL AKHBAR/LIAISON AGENCY

Sadat is assassinated by Islamic fundamentalist gunmen at the Annual Commemorative Military Parade for the 1973 Arab–Israeli war, Cairo, 6 October 1981. A number of Arab nations openly applauded his assassination.

Bei der alljährlichen Militärparade zur Erinnerung an den arabisch-israelischen Krieg von 1973 wurde Sadat am 6. Oktober 1981 in Kairo von islamischen Fundamentalisten ermordet. Einige arabische Nationen spendeten dieser Bluttat offenen Beifall.

Sadate est assassiné par des islamistes fondamentalistes lors du défilé militaire marquant la commémoration annuelle de la guerre israélo-arabe de 1973, Caire, le 6 octobre 1981. De nombreuses nations arabes approuvèrent ouvertement cet assassinat.

VOLKER CORELL/BLACK STAR/COLORIFIC!

After clashes between Sikhs and Hindus in Amritsar in June 1984, the Indian Prime Minister Indira Gandhi (above) ordered troops to storm the Golden Temple, the holiest of Sikh shrines. Four months later, Mrs Gandhi was assassinated by her own bodyguards.

Nach Zusammenstößen zwischen Hindus und Sikhs im Juni 1984 in Amritsar befahl die indische Ministerpräsidentin Indira Gandhi (oben) dem Militär, den Goldenen Tempel, das wichtigste Heiligtum der Sikhs, zu erstürmen. Vier Monate später wurde Gandhi von ihren eigenen Leibwächtern ermordet.

Après les émeutes entre Sikhs et Hindous à Amritsar en juin 1984, le Premier ministre indien Indira Gandhi (ci-dessus) ordonna à l'armée de prendre d'assaut le Temple d'or, le lieu le plus sacré des Sikhs. Quatre mois plus tard, Mme Gandhi fut assassinée par ses propres gardes du corps.

Rajiv Gandhi
(centre, in white
hat) watches over
the funeral pyre
of his mother,
Indira Gandhi,
November 1984.

Rajiv Gandhi (in der
Mitte, mit weißer
Kopfbedeckung)
an der Verbren-
nungsstätte seiner
Mutter Indira,
November 1984.

Rajiv Gandhi
(au centre, avec le
képi blanc) veille sur
le bûcher funéraire
de sa mère,
Indira Gandhi,
novembre 1984.

COLORIFIC!

Prompting the witness... Colonel Oliver North listens to his counsel
during the Iran-Contra hearings before the Joint House of
Representatives and Senate Committee, Washington, DC, May 1987.

Was soll ich sagen? Colonel Oliver North mit seinem Rechtsbeistand
während der Iran-Contra-Anhörungen des vereinten Ausschusses von
Senat und Repräsentantenhaus, Washington, D. C., Mai 1987.

Souffler la réplique au témoin ... Le colonel Oliver North écoute
son avocat durant les auditions de l'Iran-Contra devant la commission
interparlementaire de la Chambre des représentants et du Sénat,
Washington, mai 1987.

Silent witness. The Ayatollah Khomeini of Iran contemplates the future. He ruled Iran from 1979 to 1989.

Stiller Zeuge. Ayatollah Khomeini, das geistliche Oberhaupt des Iran, denkt an die Zukunft. Er regierte das Land von 1979 bis 1989.

Témoin silencieux. L'ayatollah iranien Khomeiny songe à l'avenir. Il gouverna l'Iran de 1979 à 1989.

MICHAEL COYNE/BLACK STAR/COLORIFIC!

Colonel Muammar Gaddafi attends celebrations of the 18th anniversary of the Republic of Libya, September 1987. In 1969 he had led the Free Officers Movement which overthrew the former ruler, King Idris.

Oberst Muammar Gaddafi bei den Feierlichkeiten zum 18. Jahrestag der Gründung der Republik Libyen im September 1987. 1969 führte er den Bund „freier Offiziere", der den damaligen Herrscher, König Idris, absetzte.

Le colonel Mouammar Kadhafi assiste aux célébrations du 18ᵉ anniversaire de la république de Libye, septembre 1987. En 1969, il conduisit le Mouvement des jeunes officiers qui renversa l'ancien dirigeant, le roi Idris.

President Saddam
Hussein visits the
front during the
Iran–Iraq war,
21 March 1988.
Millions had already
died in the war
which began in
September 1981.

Der irakische
Präsident Saddam
Hussein beim
Besuch der Front
während des
iranisch-irakischen
Krieges, 21. März
1988. Zu diesem
Zeitpunkt waren
bereits Millionen
in diesem Krieg
gestorben, der im
September 1981
ausgebrochen war.

Visite du président
Saddam Hussein
sur le front durant
la guerre irako-
iranienne,
le 21 mars 1988.
Des millions de
personnes avaient
déjà péri dans cette
guerre qui débuta
en septembre 1981.

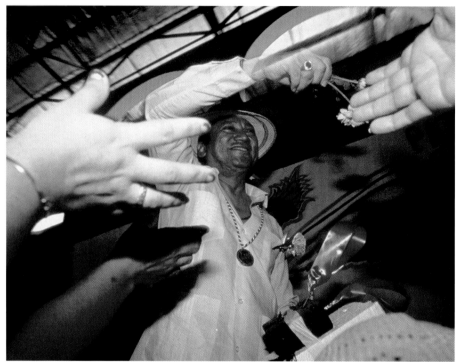

CHRISTOPHER MORRIS/BLACK STAR/COLORIFIC!

Temporary success. President Manuel Noriega celebrates the failure of a coup attempt, Panama City, October 1989. The celebrations did not last long. Noriega was finally ousted eight weeks later.

Ein Sieg auf Zeit. Präsident Manuel Noriega lässt sich im Oktober 1989 nach dem gescheiterten Putschversuch in Panama-Stadt feiern, aber seine Freude sollte nicht lange währen: Acht Wochen später wurde er abgesetzt.

Succès temporaire. Le président Manuel Noriega fête l'échec du coup d'état à Panama, octobre 1989. La fête ne dura pas longtemps. Noriega fut évincé huit semaines plus tard.

Temporary bandage. General Augusto Pinochet nurses his left hand, injured during an assassination attempt, 22 September 1986.

Bandagiert. Der chilenische Diktator Augusto Pinochet hält seine linke Hand, an der er bei einem Attentat verletzt worden war, 22. September 1986.

Pansement temporaire. Le général Augusto Pinochet soigne sa main gauche, blessée lors d'une tentative d'assassinat, le 22 septembre 1986.

ERIK DE CASTRO/REUTERS/HULTON|ARCHIVE

'Come on baby light my fire…': Imelda Marcos woos and wows her dictatorial husband, President Ferdinand Marcos, during an election campaign, Manila, 11 January 1986.

„Come on baby light my fire …" Imelda Marcos schmachtet ihren Gatten, den diktatorisch regierenden Präsidenten Ferdinand Marcos, bei einer Wahlkampfveranstaltung an, Manila, 11. Januar 1986.

« Come on baby light my fire … » : Imelda Marcos courtise et séduit son dictateur d'époux, le président Ferdinand Marcos, en campagne pour les élections, Manille, le 11 janvier 1986.

President P W Botha lays it down big time on a marimba after opening a training and work centre, Crossroads township, South Africa, 26 August 1988.

Er gibt sich volkstümlich. P. W. Botha, der Präsident des südafrikanischen Apartheid-Regimes, nach der Eröffnung eines Ausbildungs- und Arbeitszentrums in der Township Crossroads als Virtuose am Marimbaphon, 26. August 1988.

Le président P. W. Botha bat la mesure au marimba après l'inauguration d'un centre pour la formation et l'emploi dans le township de Crossroads, Afrique du Sud, le 26 août 1988.

2. Conflict
Konflikte
Les conflits

Sisters in arms. Members of the Iranian militia march through the streets of Tehran to celebrate the Day of the Woman, 24 March 1984. The war between Iran and Iraq was at its height at this time.

Frauen am Gewehr. Weibliche Angehörige der iranischen Miliz marschieren anlässlich des Tags der Frau durch die Straßen Teherans, 24. März 1984. Der Krieg zwischen Iran und Irak befand sich gerade auf dem Höhepunkt.

Sœurs d'armes. Défilé des membres de la milice dans les rues de Téhéran pour célébrer la Journée de la femme, 24 mars 1984. La guerre entre l'Iran et l'Irak était à son comble à cette époque.

2. Conflict
Konflikte
Les conflits

Forty years on from the Second World War, the world managed to avoid another global conflict. Fighting was local, rather than on the grand scale. There were wars of liberation, of revolution, of colonial greed, and between unhappy neighbours. There were bombing raids and instances of armed intervention – notably by the United States.

The Soviet Union spent lives and resources in an ultimately unsuccessful attempt to save Afghanistan from the encroaching *mujahedin*; Britain reverted to 19th-century patterns of behaviour when a handful of Argentinian scientists and soldiers landed in South Georgia; Iran and Iraq spent most of the decade in bitter dispute. There were armed insurrections in Colombia, Nicaragua, El Salvador, Chile, the Philippines, Haiti and Panama. The civil war in Angola dragged on throughout the decade. Riots erupted in South Africa, South Korea, south London, Northern Ireland and France.

In a decade of chilly catchphrases – 'second cold war', 'Soviet and US neo-colonial expansion', 'evil empire', 'ideological warfare', 'nuclear stockpiling' – it was a mercy that the anticipated holocaust between East and West did not materialise.

40 Jahre waren seit dem Zweiten Weltkrieg vergangen; es gelang, eine neue globale militärische Auseinandersetzung zu vermeiden. Aber es gab lokal begrenzte Kriege. Befreiungskriege, Revolutionskriege, Kolonialkriege, Kriege zwischen feindlichen Nachbarländern. Es gab Bombenangriffe und bewaffnete Interventionen – vor allem seitens der Vereinigten Staaten.

Die Sowjetunion verschwendete Menschenleben und Ressourcen auf den letztlich erfolglosen Versuch, Afghanistan gegen die vordringenden Mudschahedin zu halten; Großbritannien fiel auf Verhaltensmuster des 19. Jahrhunderts zurück, als eine Hand voll argentinischer Techniker und Soldaten auf Südgeorgien landeten; zwischen Iran und Irak tobte fast das gesamte Jahrzehnt hindurch ein furchtbarer Krieg. Es gab bewaffnete Aufstände in Kolumbien, Nicaragua, El Salvador, Chile, auf den Philippinen, in Haiti und Panama. Der Bürgerkrieg in Angola ging in den achtziger Jahren weiter. Zu Unruhen kam es in Südafrika, in Südkorea, im Süden Londons, in Nordirland und in Frankreich.

Es war ein Glück und eine Gnade, dass in einem Jahrzehnt der beunruhigenden Schlagworte – „zweiter Kalter Krieg", „neokoloniale Expansion der UdSSR und USA", „Reich des Bösen", „ideologische Kriegsführung", „nukleares Wettrüsten" – letztlich der befürchtete Untergang in einem Atomkrieg zwischen Ost und West ausblieb.

Quarante ans après la Seconde Guerre mondiale, le monde avait su empêcher qu'une nouvelle guerre mondiale éclate. Les conflits se développaient localement et non plus à grande échelle. Il y eut des révolutions et des guerres de libération, des guerres post-coloniales et d'autres menées entre pays voisins belliqueux. Des bombardements aériens et des interventions armées furent déclenchés, notamment par les États-Unis.

L'Union soviétique gaspilla des vies et des armes dans une ultime et vaine tentative de sauver l'Afghanistan de l'emprise moudjahidin. La Grande-Bretagne répliqua au débarquement d'une poignée de scientifiques et de soldats argentins en Géorgie du Sud, en usant de méthodes dignes du 19ᵉ siècle. L'Iran et l'Iraq se livrèrent à une guerre cruelle et quasi incessante tout au long de la décennie. Il y eut des insurrections armées en Colombie, au Nicaragua, au Salvador, au Chili, aux Philippines, en Haïti et au Panama. La guerre civile fit rage en Angola durant toute la décennie. Il y eut des émeutes en Afrique du Sud, en Corée du Sud, dans le sud de Londres, en Irlande du Nord et en France.

La décennie fut marquée par des slogans qui faisaient froid dans le dos – « deuxième guerre froide », « expansion néocoloniale des Russes et des Américains, « empire du mal », « guerre idéologique », « arsenal nucléaire » – et ce fut un miracle que le conflit qui devait éclater entre l'Est et l'Ouest ne se concrétise pas.

STRINGER/REUTERS/HULTON|ARCHIVE

Protection. A Muslim *mullah* (left) and a member of the Iranian Revolutionary Guard visit the battle zone near Oshnoviyeh in north-west Iran, 8 August 1988. Iran repeatedly claimed that the Iraqis were using chemical weapons.

Schutzmaßnahme. Ein muslimischer Mullah (links) und ein Mitglied der iranischen Revolutionsgarde besuchen die Kampfzone in der Nähe der nordwestiranischen Stadt Oshnoviyeh, 8. August 1988. Wiederholt warfen iranische Stellen dem Irak vor, chemische Waffen einzusetzen.

Protection. Un mollah musulman (à gauche) et un membre de la garde révolutionnaire iranienne en déplacement sur un champ de bataille près de Oshnoviyeh au nord-ouest de l'Iran, 8 août 1988. L'Iran affirma à maintes reprises que les Irakiens avaient recours aux armes chimiques.

Destruction. Two of the 5,000 who died when Iraqi troops used chemical weapons to bombard a Kurdish village in a region occupied by Iran. The Iran–Iraq war was the most destructive of the decade.

Zerstörung. Zwei der 5000 Toten, die ein Giftgasangriff irakischer Truppen auf ein kurdisches Dorf in der vom Iran besetzten Zone forderte. Der iranisch-irakische Krieg war die blutigste militärische Auseinandersetzung der achtziger Jahre.

Destruction. Deux des 5 000 victimes de l'armée irakienne qui utilisa des armes chimiques pour bombarder un village kurde dans une région occupée par l'Iran. La guerre irano-irakienne fut le conflit le plus meurtrier de toute la décennie.

ALFRED/LIAISON AGENCY

It was a war grotesquely old fashioned in the way it consumed young lives. (Above) A Pasdaran soldier wades through mud and silt on the Howaza battlefront. He was killed later the same day.

Dieser atavistisch geführte Krieg forderte das Leben vieler junger Männer. (Oben) Der Pasdaran-Soldat, der hier durch den Sumpf an der Front bei Howaza robbt, fiel noch am selben Tag.

Ce fut une guerre grotesque, gaspillant la vie de jeunes gens en utilisant des méthodes quasi ancestrales. (Ci-dessus) Un soldat de Pasdaran avance en rampant dans la boue et le limon sur le champ de bataille de Howaza. Il mourut ce jour-là, quelques heures plus tard.

Tragic triumph. A victorious *mullah* raises his rifle in salute as he stands above a pile of Iraqi corpses.

Tragischer Triumph. Ein siegreicher Mullah präsentiert sein Maschinengewehr; er steht über einem Haufen irakischer Leichen.

Triomphe tragique. Un mollah victorieux brandit son fusil en guise de salut, debout au-dessus de cadavres irakiens.

ALFRED/LIAISON AGENCY

Hostage situations.
(Left) Members of
the SAS successfully
raid the Iranian
Embassy in London,
5 May 1980.
(Opposite) US
hostages arrive home
after 444 days
captivity in Iran,
January 1981.

Geiselnahmen.
(Links) Angehörige
der SAS stürmen am
5. Mai 1980 mit
Erfolg die iranische
Botschaft in London.
(Gegenüberliegende
Seite) Amerikanische
Geiseln treffen
nach 444-tägiger
Gefangenschaft im
Iran zu Hause ein,
Januar 1981.

Prise d'otages.
(À gauche) Interven-
tion réussie des
membres du SAS
à l'Ambassade ira-
nienne de Londres,
5 mai 1980.
(Ci-contre) Arrivée
des otages américains
après 444 jours de
captivité en Iran,
janvier 1981.

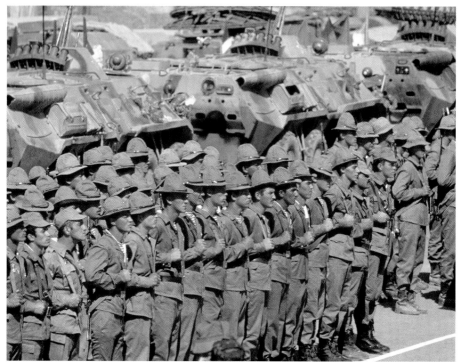

ANDY HERNANDEZ/COLORIFIC!

The Soviet Vietnam. Soldiers from the Red Army parade in Kabul in the early 1980s.
'The first thing which surprised me was the countryside, the Asian moon, the stars.
I felt like a tourist…' – a young Russian recruit in Afghanistan.

Das Vietnam der Sowjetunion. Soldaten der Roten Armee bei einer Militärparade
in Kabul zu Beginn der achtziger Jahre. „Das erste, was mich überraschte, war das
Land, der asiatische Mond, die Sterne. Ich kam mir vor wie ein Tourist …" –
Worte eines jungen russischen Rekruten in Afghanistan.

Le Viêtnam soviétique. Des soldats de l'Armée rouge défilent à Kaboul au début des
années 1980. « Ma première surprise a été le paysage, la lune asiatique, les étoiles.
Je me sentais comme un touriste … » – Témoignage d'un soldat russe en Afghanistan.

Members of the *mujahedin* on guard near their base at Jagdalak, Afghanistan, February 1987. The USSR lost more than 20,000 men, the *mujahedin* more than a million. 'You wonder what the point was', wrote a Russian conscript.

Angehörige der Mudschahedin auf Wache nahe ihrer Basis im afghanischen Jagdalak, Februar 1987. Die UdSSR verloren mehr als 20 000 Mann, die Mudschahedin mehr als eine Million. „Man fragt sich, worum es eigentlich ging", schrieb ein russischer Wehrpflichtiger.

Des moudjahidin font la garde près de leur base de Jagdalak, Afghanistan, février 1987. L'URSS perdit plus de 20 000 hommes et les moudjahidin plus d'un million. « On se demande quel est le but de cette guerre » écrivit un soldat russe.

The People's
Committees take
to the streets of
Tripoli after a
TV broadcast by
Colonel Gaddafi
following US
bombing raids
on Libya,
16 April 1986.

Die Volkskomitees
demonstrieren auf
den Straßen von
Tripolis. Oberst
Gaddafi hatte sie nach
US-amerikanischen
Bombenangriffen auf
Libyen in einer
Fernsehansprache
dazu aufgerufen,
16. April 1986.

Les comités du peuple
envahissent les rues
de Tripoli après
l'intervention
télévisée du colonel
Kadhafi consécutive
aux bombardements
aériens des Améri-
cains sur la Libye,
16 avril 1986.

PATRICK ROBERT/SIPA PRESS

A child's foot protrudes from the rubble of a building destroyed during the US raids on Libya, April 1986. The raids were in retaliation for the death of one US soldier killed in a terrorist attack on a West Berlin discotheque.

Der Fuß eines Kindes ragt aus den Trümmern eines Hauses, das während der amerikanischen Bombenangriffe auf Libyen im April 1986 zerstört wurde. Die Angriffe waren ein Vergeltungsakt für den Tod eines US-Soldaten, der bei einem Terroranschlag auf eine Westberliner Diskothek ums Leben gekommen war.

Le pied d'un enfant émergeant des ruines d'un immeuble détruit durant les raids américains en Libye, avril 1986. Ces raids furent menés par représailles suite à la mort d'un soldat américain dans un attentat terroriste contre une discothèque à Berlin-Ouest.

CHRISTOPHER MORRIS/BLACK STAR/COLORIFIC!

Policing the world. One of the 26,000 US troops who entered Panama on 20 December 1989. The fighting was unexpectedly heavy and some 1,500 people were killed.

Der Weltpolizist. Einer von 26 000 US-Soldaten, die am 20. Dezember 1989 in Panama landeten. Es kam zu unerwartet heftigen Kämpfen und circa 1500 Menschen wurden getötet.

Maintien de l'ordre mondial. Un des 26 000 soldats qui pénétrèrent au Panama le 20 décembre 1989. Les combats furent plus durs que prévus et plus de 1500 personnes furent tuées.

Before US intervention in Panama, President Noriega faced military revolt from within in 1988. This was backed by some of the civilian population with stones for bullets and tables for barricades.

Vor der US-Intervention musste sich der panamaische Präsident Noriega 1988 mit einer Militärrevolte auseinandersetzen. Einige Zivilisten versuchten, die Aufständischen mit Steinwürfen und aus Tischen errichteten Barrikaden zu unterstützen.

Avant l'intervention américaine au Panama, le président Noriega fut confronté à la révolte militaire au sein de son propre camp en 1988. Celle-ci fut soutenue par la population civile qui usa de pierres en guise de balles et de tables à défaut de barricades.

M. NAYTHONS/LIAISON AGENCY

The scene: a quiet road on the Caribbean island of Grenada. The time: October 1983. The sign reads 'Communism stops here'. The absurd pretext for the invasion was that the new regime on the island posed a threat to the security of the United States.

Schauplatz: eine ruhige Landstraße auf der Karibikinsel Grenada. Zeit: Oktober 1983. Auf dem Schild steht: „Hier endet der Kommunismus." Der absurde Vorwand für die Invasion lautete, das neue Regime der Inselrepublik bedrohe die Sicherheit der Vereinigten Staaten.

Lieu : route tranquille sur l'île de Grenade dans les Caraïbes. Date : octobre 1983. Le panneau dit « le communisme s'arrête ici ». Le prétexte absurde qui motiva l'invasion fut que le nouveau régime de l'île constituait une menace pour la sécurité des États-Unis.

An American soldier
stands guard over a
Panamanian suspect
in the aftermath
of the US invasion
to oust Noriega,
26 December 1989.

Ein US-Soldat
bewacht einen
panamaischen Ver-
dächtigen. Szene im
Zusammenhang mit
der amerikanischen
Invasion zum
Sturz Noriegas,
26. Dezember 1989.

Un soldat américain
surveille un suspect
panaméen suite à
l'invasion améri-
caine destinée à
évincer Noriega,
26 décembre 1989.

RAPHAEL GAILLARDE/LIAISON AGENCY

Prelude to Irangate. A US helicopter brings
supplies to the anti-government Contra rebels
in northern Nicaragua, April 1987. President
Reagan's support for the rebels brought him
into conflict with Congress, and eventually
led to the Irangate affair.

Das Vorspiel zur Iran-Contra-Affäre. Ein
US-Hubschrauber beliefert die Contras, die
gegen die sandinistische Regierung im Norden Nicaraguas operierten, mit Nachschub,
April 1987. Die Unterstützung für die Rebel-
len brachte Präsident Reagan in Konflikt mit
dem Kongress und führte schließlich zur Iran-
Contra-Affäre.

Prélude à l'Irangate. Approvisionnement des
Contra, rebelles antigouvernementaux, par
un hélicoptère américain dans le nord du
Nicaragua, avril 1987. Le soutien du président Reagan à la cause des rebelles déclencha
l'hostilité du Congrès avant que l'affaire ne
se transforme en scandale de l'Irangate.

Obeying the power that arms them. A training camp for Nicaraguan Contra guerrillas, somewhere in Honduras, February 1989. The civil war was ebbing to a close and towards peaceful elections one year later.

Der Macht gehorchend, die sie bewaffnete. Trainingslager der nicaraguanischen Contras irgendwo in Honduras, Februar 1989. Der Bürgerkrieg flaute ab; ein Jahr später fanden freie Wahlen in dem mittelamerikanischen Land statt.

Soumission au pouvoir qui les arme. Camp d'entraînement pour les guerrillos de la Contra nicaraguayenne, quelque part au Honduras, février 1989. La guerre civile touchait à sa fin et des élections purent avoir lieu dans le calme un an plus tard.

Mocking the hand that feeds them. Athletic adolescents leap to spray revolutionary slogans on a giant McDonald's billboard in El Salvador, 15 March 1989. The presidential elections were a few days away.

Hohn und Spott für die Schutzmacht. Drahtige Jugendliche springen hoch, um revolutionäre Slogans auf eine riesige Werbetafel von McDonald's zu sprühen, El Salvador, 15. März 1989. Ein paar Tage später fanden Präsidentschaftswahlen statt.

Railler la main qui les nourrit. Des adolescents athlétiques sautent haut pour taguer des slogans révolutionnaires sur le panneau géant d'un Mac Donald au Salvador, le 15 mars 1989, quelques jours avant les élections présidentielles.

Water cannon in action on the streets of Santiago, Chile, 13 September 1988.
The security forces had been called out to disperse crowds protesting at the use
of torture by the Pinochet regime.

Wasserwerfer im Einsatz in den Straßen Santiago de Chiles, 13. September 1988.
Die Sicherheitskräfte sollten die Menge zerstreuen, die gegen die Folterpraxis
des Pinochet-Regimes demonstrierte.

Canons à eau dans les rues de Santiago, Chili, 13 septembre 1988. L'armée fut
appelée en renfort pour disperser la foule qui protestait contre l'usage de la
torture par le régime de Pinochet.

CHRISTOPHER MORRIS/BLACK STAR/COLORIFIC!

A month later, full-scale riots broke out in Santiago following a plebiscite in which Chileans voted for an end to the fifteen-year dictatorship of General Augusto Pinochet.

Einen Monat später brachen in Santiago de Chile Unruhen aus. Vorausgegangen war eine Volksabstimmung, in der sich die chilenischen Wähler für ein Ende der seit 15 Jahren währenden Diktatur des Generals Augusto Pinochet aussprachen.

Un mois plus tard, d'importantes émeutes éclatèrent à Santiago suite au plébiscite, voté par les Chiliens, pour la fin de la dictature du général Augusto Pinochet qui durait depuis 15 ans.

EL ESPECTADOR/SIPA PRESS

Soldiers and tanks surround the Palace of Justice, home of the Supreme
Court of Colombia, 8 November 1985. The building, in the centre of
Bogota, had been occupied by the revolutionary leftist group M-19.

Soldaten und Panzer umstellen den Justizpalast, den Sitz des Obersten
Gerichtes Kolumbiens, 8. November 1985. Das Gebäude im Zentrum
Bogotas war von Angehörigen der linken Revolutionsbewegung M-19
besetzt worden.

Soldats et chars encerclent le palais de justice, siège de la Cour suprême de
Colombie, le 8 novembre 1985. Situé dans le centre de Bogota, le bâtiment
était occupé par le groupe révolutionnaire d'extrême-gauche, M-19.

When the Palace was taken by storm more than 100 people were killed, including the President of the Supreme Court and thirty members of M-19.

Bei der Erstürmung des Justizpalastes wurden mehr als 100 Menschen getötet, darunter der Präsident des Obersten Gerichtes und 30 Mitglieder von M-19.

Le palais fut pris d'assaut, causant la mort de plus de 100 personnes, dont le président de la Cour suprême et trente membres du M-19.

EL ESPECTADOR/SIPA PRESS

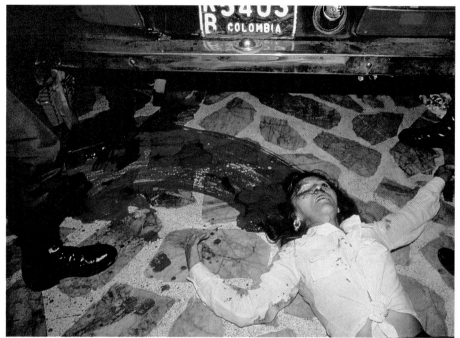

Life and death on the streets of Medellín, Colombia, 1989: the victim of a gang who came through a bedroom window, tortured and raped her before finally killing her.

Leben und Sterben in Medellín, Kolumbien, 1989. Die Gangster kamen durch das Schlafzimmerfenster. Sie folterten und vergewaltigten diese Frau, bevor sie sie schließlich umbrachten.

Vie et mort dans les rues de Medellín, Colombie, 1989 : victime d'un gang qui, après avoir fait irruption dans sa chambre par la fenêtre, la tortura et la viola avant de l'achever.

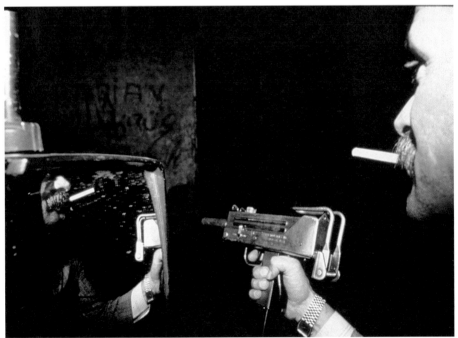

Armed civil officers of the DOC (Colombian security forces) on night patrol. The photographer described his arrival in Medellín as entering 'the gates of hell'.

Bewaffnete Beamte der kolumbianischen Sicherheitskräfte (DOC) in Zivil beim nächtlichen Einsatz. Der Fotograf meinte später, in Medellín sei er sich „wie in der Hölle" vorgekommen.

Des policiers en civil armés de la DOC (forces de sécurité colombiennes) en patrouille de nuit. Le photographe décrivit son arrivée dans Medellín comme une entrée par les « portes de l'enfer ».

The Royal Navy
frigate HMS *Antelope*
is torn apart by an
Argentinian bomb,
San Carlos Bay,
Falkland Islands,
24 February 1982.

Die Fregatte
HMS *Antelope* der
britischen Kriegs-
marine wird von
einer argentinischen
Bombe in Stücke
gerissen, San Carlos
Bay, Falklandinseln,
24. Februar 1982.

La frégate de la
marine royale britan-
nique *Antelope*
explose sous le choc
d'une bombe argen-
tine, Baie de San
Carlos, îles Falkland,
le 24 février 1982.

MARTIN CLEAVER/PA

Survivors from HMS *Sir Galahad* are hauled ashore at Bluff Cove, East Falkland, 29 June 1982.
'A red alert went. We hit the deck and I saw this great orange and red streak. Trouble was, I
watched and didn't protect my face…' – Simon Weston.

Überlebende des britischen Kriegsschiffs HMS *Sir Galahad* werden in Bluff Cove, Ostfalkland,
an Land gesetzt, 29. Juni 1982. „Wir schlugen zu Boden, ich sah den grellen roten Lichtblitz.
Das Problem war, ich guckte hin und schützte mein Gesicht nicht …" – Simon Weston.

Des survivants du bâtiment naval *Sir Galahad* sont tirés vers le rivage à Bluff Cove, à l'est
de Falkland, le 29 juin 1982. «Y'a eu une alerte rouge. On est tombé sur le pont et j'ai vu ce
grand éclair orange et rouge. Le problème c'est que j'ai regardé au lieu de me protéger le
visage … » Témoignage de Simon Weston.

TOM SMITH/EXPRESS NEWSPAPERS/HULTON|ARCHIVE

British paratroopers carry a wounded soldier to safety
while under fire on Mount Longdon during the Falklands
campaign, 12–13 July 1982.

Britische Fallschirmjäger bringen einen verwundeten
Kameraden in Sicherheit, während sie beschossen werden,
Mount Longdon, im Falklandkrieg, 12.–13. Juli 1982.

Des parachutistes britanniques transportent un soldat
blessé vers un lieu sûr alors que la bataille fait rage sur
le Mont Longdon durant la guerre des Falkland,
12–13 juillet 1982.

PA

The spoils of war. The fields around Goose Green are littered with the abandoned helmets of the Argentine soldiers who surrendered to British Falklands Task Force troops, 21 May 1982.

Siegestrophäen. Stahlhelme auf den Feldern um Goose Green. Ihre Besitzer waren argentinische Soldaten, die sich den britischen Einsatz-truppen auf den Falklandinseln ergeben hatten, 21. Mai 1982.

Les gâchis de la guerre. Les champs autour de Goose Green sont jon-chés de casques abandonnés par les soldats argentins qui se sont rendus aux soldats du corps expéditionnaire des Falkland britanniques, 21 mai 1982.

HULTON|ARCHIVE

British troops escort an Argentinian prisoner of war. He was one of the lucky ones.
More than 1,000 men died serving the governments of Britain and Argentina in their
squabble over a group of islands at the bottom of the world.

Britische Soldaten führen einen argentinischen Gefangenen ab. Er hatte Glück.
Insgesamt fielen auf beiden Seiten mehr als 1000 Mann bei dem Streit zwischen der
britischen und der argentinischen Regierung um eine Inselgruppe am Ende der Welt.

Prisonnier de guerre argentin sous escorte britannique. Il fait partie de ceux qui ont
eu la chance de ne pas y laisser leur vie. Plus d'un millier d'hommes moururent au
service des gouvernements britannique et argentin, qui entrèrent en conflit pour
quelques îles situées au bout du monde.

Sikhs surrender to units of the Indian army on the outskirts of the Golden Temple, Amritsar, early in 1984.

Sikhs ergeben sich vor dem Goldenen Tempel von Amritsar Einheiten der indischen Armee, Anfang 1984.

Des Sikhs se rendent aux forces de l'armée indienne non loin du Temple d'or, Amritsar, début 1984.

PABLO BARTHOLOMEW/LIAISON AGENCY

After the Sikh movement for greater political and religious autonomy led to clashes with Hindus, the Indian Prime Minister Indira Gandhi ordered troops into Amritsar. More than 1,000 people were killed in subsequent fighting.

Nachdem es aufgrund des Strebens der Sikhs nach größerer politischer und religiöser Autonomie zu Zusammenstößen mit den Hindus gekommen war, schickte die indische Ministerpräsidentin Indira Gandhi Truppen nach Amritsar. Bei den anschließenden Kämpfen wurden mehr als 1000 Menschen getötet.

Suite au mouvement sikh en faveur d'une plus grande autonomie politique et religieuse qui donna lieu à des affrontements avec les hindous, le Premier ministre indien, Indira Gandhi, ordonna à l'armée de pénétrer dans Amritsar. Plus de 1000 personnes furent tuées lors des combats qui en résultèrent.

NICKELSBERG/LIAISON AGENCY

Intercommunal violence swept Sri Lanka in the early 1980s. President Junius Jayawardine gave wide-ranging powers to his security forces to combat Tamil separatist groups. (Above) Civilians are caught in the crossfire between rival gangs.

Gewalttätige Auseinandersetzungen zwischen den Volksgruppen suchten Sri Lanka zu Beginn der achtziger Jahre heim. Präsident Junius Jayawardine räumte seinen Sicherheitskräften weitgehende Vollmachten ein, um die tamilischen Separatisten zu bekämpfen. (Oben) Zivilisten im Kreuzfeuer zwischen den bewaffneten Gruppen.

Des violences intercommunautaires ravagèrent le Sri Lanka au début des années 1980. Le président Junius Jayawardine accorda des pouvoirs étendus aux forces armées pour combattre les groupes séparatistes tamouls. (Ci-dessous) Civils piégés par un échange de tirs entre gangs rivaux.

Fire, looting and murder erupted on the streets of Colombo (above), and thousands of Tamils fled to the north of the island. In 1983 alone, some 380 people were killed in battles between Tamils and Singhalese.

Brand, Plünderung und Mord in den Straßen Colombos (oben); Tausende von Tamilen flohen in den Norden der Insel. Allein im Jahr 1983 starben etwa 380 Menschen in den Kämpfen zwischen Tamilen und Singhalesen.

Incendies, pillages et assassinats firent irruption dans les rues de Colombo (ci-dessus) et des milliers de Tamouls s'enfuirent dans le nord de l'île. Pour la seule année de 1983, quelque 380 personnes furent tuées au cours d'affrontements entre Tamouls et Cinghalais.

Not for the first or the last time, violence breaks out in the Occupied Territories. Palestinian women and children prepare to do battle with Israeli forces.

Nicht zum ersten und nicht zum letzten Mal kam es in den besetzten Gebieten zu Gewaltausbrüchen. Palästinensische Frauen und Kinder bereiten sich auf den Kampf mit den israelischen Besatzungsstreitkräften vor.

Ce n'est ni la première ni la dernière fois que la violence éclate dans les territoires occupés. Des enfants et des femmes palestiniens se préparent à défier l'armée israélienne.

ARAL/SIPA PRESS

A mother hurries to safety across the rubble of Beirut during an Israeli bombardment, June 1982. The Israeli invasion of 90,000 troops, code-named 'Peace for Galilee', was intended to drive out the PLO. It failed.

Eine Mutter eilt durch den Schutt, um sich und ihr Kind vor einem israelischen Bombenangriff in Sicherheit zu bringen, Beirut, Juni 1982. Der israelische Einmarsch in den Libanon, Deckname „Frieden für Galiläa", an dem 90 000 Mann beteiligt waren, hatte das Ziel, die PLO zu vertreiben. Er scheiterte.

Mère courant parmi les gravats de Beyrouth pour se mettre à l'abri pendant un bombardement israélien, juin 1982. L'invasion israélienne conduite avec 90 000 soldats, ayant pour nom de code « paix en Galilée », fut menée pour terrasser l'OLP. Elle échoua.

Ali Jawad is executed by the Amal militia in south Beirut,
30 November 1986. He had been accused of planting bombs
that had killed eight people and injured forty-five others in Shiite
neighbourhoods.

Ali Jawad wird von Angehörigen der Amal-Miliz im Süden
Beiruts hingerichtet, 30. November 1986. Der Mann war
beschuldigt worden, die Sprengsätze gelegt zu haben, die im
Schiitenviertel acht Menschen getötet und 45 verletzt hatten.

Exécution d'Ali Jawad par la milice d'Amal à Beyrouth sud,
le 30 novembre 1986. Il était accusé d'avoir posé des bombes
dans les quartiers chiites, faisant huit victimes et 45 blessés.

A civilian carries a baby from the wreckage of a building in west Beirut, 1983. By this time, anarchy reigned in what was left of the city, with fighting between Druze militiamen, Christians, units of the Lebanese army and Shiite fighters.

Ein Zivilist rettet ein Baby aus den Trümmern eines Gebäudes im Westen Beiruts, 1983. Zu dieser Zeit herrschte Anarchie in dem, was von der libanesischen Hauptstadt übrig geblieben war. Drusen, Schiiten, Christen und Einheiten der libanesischen Armee bekämpften sich wechselseitig.

Un civil porte un bébé dégagé des ruines d'un immeuble à Beyrouth ouest, 1983. À cette époque, l'anarchie régnait dans la ville en grande partie détruite et livrée aux combats entre milices druzes, chrétiens, unités de l'armée libanaise et combattants chiites.

1985 was an unhappy year in South Africa. It was the 25th anniversary of the Sharpeville Massacre, and violence erupted yet again. (Above) Mourners give the African salute at a funeral in Kwa-Thena, July 1985.

1985 war ein unglückliches Jahr für Südafrika. Am 25. Jahrestag des Massakers von Sharpeville brachen erneut Gewalttätigkeiten aus. (Oben) Trauernde geben Opfern das letzte Geleit, Begräbnis in Kwa-Thena, Juli 1985.

1985 fut une année triste en Afrique du Sud. Lors du 25ᵉ anniversaire des massacres de Sharpeville, la violence éclata à nouveau. (Ci-dessus) Les familles des victimes font le salut africain lors des funérailles à Kwa-Thena, juillet 1985.

Desmond Tutu,
Bishop of Johannes-
burg and winner of
the 1984 Nobel
Peace Prize, speaks at
the same funeral.

Auf der Beerdigung
spricht Desmond
Tutu, der Bischof
von Johannesburg,
der 1984 den
Friedensnobelpreis
erhalten hatte.

Desmond Tutu,
cardinal de
Johannesburg et
détenteur du prix
Nobel de la paix de
1984, prend la
parole lors de ces
mêmes funérailles.

Black on white. Angry black strikers turn on their attackers after the South African police fired tear-gas canisters at a crowd in the Johannesburg suburb of Doorfontein, 22 April 1987.

Schwarz gegen Weiß. Wütende schwarze Streikende gehen gegen ihre Kontrahenten vor, nachdem die südafrikanische Polizei Tränengas gegen die Menge in der Johannesburger Vorstadt Doorfontein eingesetzt hatte, 22. April 1987.

Noir sur blanc. Des grévistes noirs en colère se retournent contre leurs attaquants après que la police sud-africaine a procédé à des tirs de gaz lacrymogène sur la foule à Doorfontein, une banlieue de Johannesburg, le 22 avril 1987.

White on black. Two members of the South African security forces lay into a young black on the street in one of the townships around Capetown. It was a time of escalating violence throughout South Africa.

Weiß gegen Schwarz. Zwei Angehörige der südafrikanischen Sicherheitskräfte prügeln auf einen jungen Schwarzen in einer der um Kapstadt gelegenen Townships ein. In jener Zeit eskalierte überall in Südafrika die Gewalt.

Blanc sur noir. Deux membres des forces de sécurité sud-africaines s'en prennent à un jeune noir dans une rue d'un de ces townships qui entourent Capetown. Ce fut une époque durant laquelle la violence augmenta, se propageant dans toute l'Afrique du Sud.

JOHN GUNSTON/SIPA PRESS

War and deprivation. Female recruits undergo basic training to enable them to take their part in the civil war that ravaged Ethiopia during the 1980s. Women joined both Christian and Muslim armies.

Krieg und Elend. Weibliche Rekruten bei der Grundausbildung, die sie zur Beteiligung an dem Bürgerkrieg befähigen soll, der in den achtziger Jahren in Äthiopien wütete. Es gab weibliche Soldaten sowohl in christlichen als auch in muslimischen Truppenverbänden.

Guerre et privation. Entraînement de base pour des recrues féminines qui s'apprêtent à jouer un rôle dans la guerre civile qui ravagea l'Éthiopie durant les années 1980. Les femmes s'enrôlèrent dans les armées chrétienne et musulmane.

Although much of Africa suffered drought and famine in the 1980s, it was the plight of Ethiopia which engaged the world's attention. (Above) Starving refugees wait patiently for the next distribution of food, water and medical aid, 1985.

Zwar herrschte in den achtziger Jahren in vielen Teilen Afrikas Dürre und Hunger, aber die Situation in Äthiopien erschütterte die Weltöffentlichkeit besonders stark. (Oben) Hungerflüchtlinge warten in einem Auffanglager geduldig auf die nächste Verteilung von Nahrungsmitteln, Wasser und Medikamenten, 1985.

Au cours de cette décennie, l'Afrique entière souffrit de sécheresse et de famine, mais ce fut la tragédie de l'Éthiopie qui attira l'attention du monde. (Ci-dessus) Des réfugiés mourants de faim attendent patiemment la prochaine distribution de nourriture, d'eau et de médicaments, 1985.

A Sudanese policeman attempts to hold back
hundreds of starving refugees, 15 July 1985.
The crowd began to surge forward the
moment a small amount of relief grain
arrived from the Save the Children Fund.

Ein sudanesischer Polizist versucht, eine
Menge von Hunderten hungernder Flücht-
linge in Schach zu halten, 15. Juli 1985.
Die Menge setzte sich in Bewegung, als eine
kleine Hilfslieferung des Save the Children
Fund im Lager eintraf.

Un policier soudanais tente de contenir
les centaines de réfugiés affamés, le
15 juillet 1985. La foule déferla aussitôt après
la livraison d'une aide humanitaire dérisoire
organisée par Save the Children Fund.

PA

Some of the 30,000 women who formed a ring of peace round the US air
force base at Greenham Common, England, on 12 December 1982.
Men were excluded, and told to run the crèche and prepare the food.

30 000 Frauen bildeten am 12. Dezember 1982 eine Menschenkette um
den US-Luftwaffenstützpunkt Greenham Common, England. Bei dieser
Aktion waren Männer ausgeschlossen, sie kümmerten sich um die Kinder
und das Essen.

Quelques-unes des 30 000 femmes qui firent un cercle de paix autour
de la base aérienne américaine de Greenham Common en Angleterre,
le 12 décembre 1982. Les hommes en furent exclus et priés de s'occuper
des enfants et de faire la cuisine.

DAVEY/DAILY EXPRESS/HULTON|ARCHIVE

Police surround striking miners as 'blackleg' drivers deliver fuel to a power station at the height of the miners' dispute, 1984. It was seen by many as a heroic if bitter last stand by organised labour in Britain and, ultimately, as a betrayal by the Government.

Polizisten kesseln streikende Bergarbeiter ein, während streikbrechende Fahrer auf dem Höhepunkt des Bergarbeiterstreiks Kohle zu einem Kraftwerk bringen, 1984. In diesem Streik sahen viele den heroischen letzten Kampf der organisierten Arbeiterschaft Großbritanniens und gleichzeitig einen Verrat der Thatcher-Regierung.

La police encercle les mineurs en grève tandis que des « jaunes » livrent du carburant à une centrale électrique alors que le conflit des mineurs atteignait son paroxysme, 1984. Pour beaucoup, cette grève fut vécue comme le dernier acte à la fois héroïque et plein d'amertume des syndicats avant d'être perçue comme une trahison de la part du gouvernement.

A policeman drags
a protester away
from a rally by the
extreme right wing
National Front Party,
Lewisham, south
London,
21 April 1980.

Ein Polizist führt
einen Demonstranten
ab. Szene von einem
Krawall, den die
rechtsextreme
National Front in
Lewisham im Süden
Londons ausgelöst
hatte, 21. April 1980.

Un policier traîne un
manifestant loin d'un
rassemblement tenu
par le National Front
Party, mouvement
d'extrême droite,
à Lewisham, au
sud de Londres,
le 21 avril 1980.

GRAHAM TURNER/KEYSTONE/HULTON|ARCHIVE

KEYSTONE/HULTON|ARCHIVE

Meanwhile, in Toxteth… A policeman stands silhouetted against blazing buildings following race riots in the Liverpool suburb of Toxteth, July 1981. It was the first time the police had used CS gas on mainland Britain.

Unterdessen in Toxteth … Die Silhouette eines Polizisten zeichnet sich vor Gebäuden ab, die nach Unruhen in der Liverpooler Vorstadt Toxteth im Juli 1981 in Brand gesteckt worden waren. Es war das erste Mal, dass die Polizei in Großbritannien das Reizgas CS einsetzte.

Pendant ce temps, à Toxteth … La silhouette d'un policier se détache des habitations qui brûlent suite à des émeutes raciales à Toxteth, banlieue de Liverpool, juillet 1981. Pour la première fois en Grande-Bretagne, la police eut recours au gaz lacrymogène.

Keeping up the bad work…
Members of the Ku Klux Klan
raise the fiery cross at Stone
Mountain, Georgia,
September 1985.

Ihr Irrsinn hört nicht auf …
Mitglieder des Ku-Klux-Klan
errichten brennende Kreuze auf
dem Stone Mountain, Georgia,
September 1985.

Poursuite du sale travail …
Des membres du Ku Klux Klan
dressent leurs croix en flammes à
Stone Mountain, Georgie,
septembre 1985.

3. All fall down
Der Zusammenbruch des Ostblocks
Tout s'écroule

More fun than lessons. A pupil from a West Berlin school chips away at the Berlin Wall, 14 November 1989. Teachers organised field trips so that their classes could take home souvenir pieces of the Wall.

Spaß statt Schule. Ein Westberliner Schulkind betätigt sich als „Mauerspecht", 14. November 1989. Lehrer organisierten Klassenausflüge zur Berliner Mauer, damit sich die Kinder ihr Stück des Bauwerks als Souvenir mit nach Hause nehmen konnten.

Plus amusant que les cours. Une élève d'une école de Berlin-Ouest ébrèche au marteau le mur de Berlin, 14 novembre 1989. Les instituteurs organisèrent des excursions scolaires pour permettre à leurs classes de ramener à la maison des morceaux du mur en guise de souvenir.

3. All fall down
Der Zusammenbruch des Ostblocks
Tout s'écroule

When it came, the end was swift. For forty years or more, Eastern Europe had looked to the Soviet Union for everything – subsidies, protection, guidance, regulation, oppression, control. The monolithic structure had trembled occasionally, as in 1956 and again in 1968, but the 'evil empire' of Reagan's imagination seemed set to last forever.

In 1980 shipyard workers from Gdansk, Poland, led by Lech Walesa, forced their government to acknowledge the rights of free trade unions. Over the next ten years Walesa and the Solidarity movement nibbled away at the state's powers. There was unrest in Czechoslovakia, Romania, Hungary and East Germany. Incapable of change, Communist leaders responded by clamping down, making arrests, restricting freedom. The greatest impetus for reform came from the Soviet Union itself. In March 1985 Mikhail Gorbachev was appointed general secretary of the Communist Party. He brought a new directness, not least with his habit of turning to his advisers after a briefing and asking: 'Do you really believe what you're telling me?' The writing was on the Wall.

Schließlich kam das Ende schnell. Über 40 Jahre lang hatte Osteuropa von der Sowjetunion alles zu erwarten – Hilfe, Schutz, Anleitung, Gängelung, Unterdrückung, Kontrolle. Der Monolith war zwar manchmal ins Wanken geraten, so 1956 und 1968, doch schien es, als ob Reagans „Reich des Bösen" bis in alle Ewigkeit weiter bestehen würde.

1980 erzwangen die von Lech Walesa geführten Werftarbeiter im polnischen Danzig von ihrer Regierung die Zulassung freier Gewerkschaften. In den folgenden zehn Jahren arbeiteten die Gewerkschaft Solidarität und Walesa verbissen gegen die Staatsmacht. Es gab Zeichen der Unzufriedenheit in der Tschechoslowakei, in Rumänien, Ungarn und der DDR. Unfähig, die drohenden Veränderungen anzuerkennen, wehrten sich die kommunistischen Führer mit Unterdrückungen, Verhaftungen und Einschränkungen der Freiheit. Der größte Reformwille ging von der Sowjetunion selbst aus. Im März 1985 wurde Michail Gorbatschow zum Generalsekretär der KPdSU ernannt. Er schlug einen neuen Weg ein. Das zeigte schon seine Frage an seine Berater, nachdem diese ihm Bericht erstattet hatten: „Glauben Sie wirklich, was Sie mir da erzählen?" Die Flammenschrift stand schon an der Wand.

Quand l'heure fut venue, la fin arriva rapidement. Pendant plus de quarante ans, l'Europe de l'Est avait été sous la coupe de l'Union soviétique à tout point de vue – subsides, protection, conseils, lois, oppression, répression. La structure monolithique avait parfois tremblé, comme en 1956 puis en 1968, mais cet « empire du mal », celui qui nourrissait l'imaginaire de Reagan, semblait établi pour durer infiniment.

En 1980, des ouvriers des chantiers navals de Gdansk en Pologne, menés par Lech Walesa, forcèrent le gouvernement à reconnaître le droit à l'existence de syndicats libres. Au cours des dix années qui suivirent, Walesa et le mouvement Solidarité égratignèrent le pouvoir de l'État. Des troubles apparaissaient en Tchécoslovaquie, en Roumanie, en Hongrie et en Allemagne de l'Est. Incapables de changement, les dirigeants communistes répondirent par la répression, les arrestations arbitraires et les restrictions de liberté. La plus grande impulsion de réforme vint de l'Union soviétique elle-même. En mars 1985, Mikhaïl Gorbatchev fut nommé secrétaire général du parti communiste. Il introduisit un franc-parler qui était nouveau, notamment avec son habitude de terminer une réunion en demandant à ses conseillers : « Croyez-vous vraiment ce que vous me dites ? » La réponse inéluctable allait s'écrire sur le mur de Berlin.

Glasnost reaches out. Three years after coming to power in the Soviet Union, Mikhail Gorbachev (centre, arm outstretched) visits Poland, July 1988. Behind him, in dark glasses, stands General Jaruzelski.

Glasnost greift um sich. Drei Jahre nach seinem Machtantritt besucht der sowjetische Parteichef Michail Gorbatschow (Mitte, mit ausgestreckter Hand) Polen, Juli 1988. Hinter ihm, mit Sonnenbrille, der polnische Staatschef General Jaruzelski.

La main tendue de la glasnost. Trois ans après son arrivée au pouvoir en Union soviétique, Mikhaïl Gorbatchev (au centre, bras tendu) se rend en Pologne, juillet 1988. Derrière lui, en lunettes noires, se tient le général Jaruzelski.

TASS/LEHTIKUVA OY/COLORIFIC!

Perestroika from the shop floor up. Gorbachev converses with a worker at the Likhachev auto plant, Moscow. His leadership was regarded by many as a breath of fresh air – intelligent, efficient, reforming, all that previous leaders had not been.

Perestroika an der Werkbank. Gorbatschow im Gespräch mit einer Arbeiterin der Moskauer Autofabrik Lichatschow. Unter Gorbatschows Führung wehte ein neuer Wind, so empfanden viele: Er war intelligent, effizient und reformwillig, Eigenschaften, die die früheren Führer hatten vermissen lassen.

La perestroïka du bas vers le haut. Gorbatchev s'entretient avec une ouvrière de l'usine de voitures de Likhachev à Moscou. Sa façon de diriger fut considérée par beaucoup comme un bol d'air frais – intelligent, efficace, réformateur, des qualités qui avaient fait défaut à ses prédécesseurs.

Student demonstrators jubilantly wave the flag of freedom in Tiananmen Square, Beijing, China, May 1989.

Jubelnde Studenten mit der Freiheitsfahne auf dem Platz des Himmlischen Friedens, Peking, China, Mai 1989.

Jubilation des étudiants et manifestants qui parviennent à déployer le drapeau de la liberté sur la Place Tiananmen à Pékin en Chine, mai 1989.

MICHAEL COYNE/BLACK STAR/COLORIFIC!

The demonstration was a spontaneous expression of dissatisfaction with China's ageing leadership and lack of democratic reform. Students and radicals took up what amounted to permanent occupation of the square, until the tanks moved in.

Die Demonstration war ein spontaner Ausdruck der Unzufriedenheit mit Chinas alternder Führung und ihrer Verweigerung demokratischer Reformen. Studenten und Radikale besetzten den Platz und blieben dort, bis die Panzer kamen.

La manifestation fut un mouvement spontané de protestation contre les dirigeants chinois vieillissants et le manque de réforme démocratique. Étudiants et activistes entreprirent d'occuper en permanence la Place Tiananmen jusqu'à l'arrivée des chars.

ARTHUR TSANG/REUTERS/HULTON|ARCHIVE

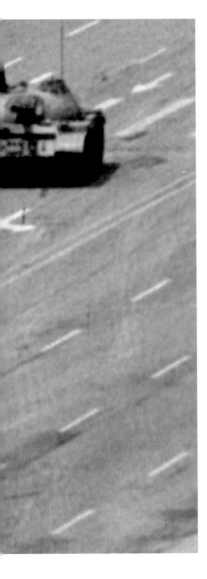

People versus power, Tiananmen Square, 5 June 1989. The man did not move; the tanks edged round him.

Das Volk und die Staatsmacht. Platz des Himmlischen Friedens, 5. Juni 1989. Der Mann blieb, wo er war; die Panzer fuhren um ihn herum.

Le peuple contre le pouvoir, Place Tiananmen, le 5 juin 1989. L'homme ne bougea pas, les chars le contournèrent.

Kiss of death.
Mikhail Gorbachev
(centre, right)
embraces East
German leader Erich
Honecker at the end
of the German
Communist Party
Conference,
East Berlin,
18 April 1986.

Der Todeskuss.
Michail Gorbatschow
(Mitte, rechts) beim
Bruderkuss mit
Erich Honecker,
Generalsekretär des
ZK der SED und
Staatsratsvorsitzender
der DDR, am Ende
des SED-Parteitags in
Ostberlin,
18. April 1986.

Le baiser de la mort.
Mikhaïl Gorbatchev
(au centre, à droite)
embrasse le dirigeant
est-allemand Erich
Honecker à la
clôture de la
Conférence du
parti communiste
allemand, Berlin-Est,
le 18 avril 1986.

East German guards watch impassively as Berliners batter the Wall near the Brandenburg Gate, Berlin, 10 November 1989.

DDR-Grenzposten schauen teilnahmslos zu, während die Berliner in der Nähe des Brandenburger Tors der Mauer zu Leibe rücken, Berlin, 10. November 1989.

Les soldats est-allemands observent, impassibles, les Berlinois qui détruisent le mur près de la porte de Brandebourg, à Berlin, le 10 novembre 1989.

DAVID BRAUCHLI/REUTERS/HULTON|ARCHIVE

EPA/PA

By the following day, the Wall had been breached, leaving a gap through which tens of thousands of citizens from East Germany streamed into West Berlin. A hated symbol of division had finally been destroyed.

Am folgenden Tag war der Durchbruch geschafft, und Zehntausende strömten aus Ostdeutschland nach Westberlin. Das verhasste Symbol der deutschen Teilung war endlich gefallen.

Le jour suivant, une brèche fut ouverte dans le mur permettant ainsi à des dizaines de milliers de citoyens d'Allemagne de l'Est de s'y engouffrer pour rejoindre Berlin-Ouest. Ce symbole de division tant haï était enfin tombé.

Day trip to freedom. A procession of Trabant cars passes Checkpoint Charlie heading west, 10 November 1989.

Tagesreisen in die Freiheit. Trabanten-Schlange am Check-point Charlie, Berlin, 10. November 1989.

Excursion d'un jour vers la liberté. File de voitures Trabant faisant la queue au Checkpoint Charlie pour passer à l'Ouest, le 10 novembre 1989.

They came to visit friends and relatives, to stroll along the Kurfürstendamm, to celebrate the death of a 28-year-old monster, or simply to assure themselves that the Wall really had been breached.

Sie kamen, um Freunde und Verwandte zu besuchen, über den Kurfürstendamm zu bummeln, den Tod des Monsters zu bejubeln, das 28 Jahre existiert hatte, oder einfach nur, um sich davon zu überzeugen, dass die Mauer tatsächlich gefallen war.

Ils vinrent pour rendre visite aux amis et à la famille, pour se promener sur le Kurfürstendamm, pour fêter la mort d'un monstre vieux de 28 ans, ou tout simplement pour s'assurer que le mur était bel et bien tombé.

On 9 November, the East German Government announced that 'citizens are free to travel'. Two days later the floodgates opened.

Am 9. November gewährte die Regierung der DDR ihren Bürgern die Reisefreiheit. Zwei Tage später gab es kein Halten mehr.

Le 9 novembre, le gouvernement est-allemand annonça que les « citoyens étaient libres de voyager ». Deux jours plus tard, les vannes étaient ouvertes.

EPA/PA

MICHAEL URBAN/REUTERS/HULTON|ARCHIVE

Joy and celebration at the Brandenburg Gate, 22 December 1989. Christmas came early to Berlin. A month earlier, the mayor of West Berlin had declared: 'The Germans are the happiest people in the world today.' The euphoria continued.

Jubel am Brandenburger Tor, 22. Dezember 1989. Weihnachten fand dieses Jahr in Berlin früher statt. Einen Monat zuvor hatte der Regierende Bürgermeister Westberlins erklärt: „Die Deutschen sind heute das glücklichste Volk in der Welt." Die Begeisterung hielt an.

Joie et fête à la porte de Brandebourg, le 22 décembre 1989. Noël arriva prématurément à Berlin. Un mois plus tôt, le maire de Berlin-Ouest avait déclaré : « Aujourd'hui, les Allemands sont les gens les plus heureux du monde. » L'euphorie n'était pas retombée.

CHESNOT/SIPA PRESS

Before the Wall came down. Though events in Berlin attracted much attention, East Germans were on the move elsewhere. For many the route to the West was through Czechoslovakia. (Above) East German refugees enter Prague, November 1989.

Vor dem Fall der Mauer. Ehe die Ereignisse in Berlin die Aufmerksamkeit auf sich zogen, waren die Ostdeutschen bereits in Bewegung. Für viele führte der Weg nach Westdeutschland über die Tschechoslowakei. (Oben) Ostdeutsche Flüchtlinge in Prag, November 1989.

Avant la chute du mur. C'était principalement ce qui se passait à Berlin qui attirait l'attention, mais il y avait des mouvements d'Allemands de l'Est ailleurs aussi. Pour beaucoup, la route vers l'Ouest passait par la Tchécoslovaquie. (Ci-dessus) Réfugiés d'Allemagne de l'Est à Prague, novembre 1989.

GUNAYDIN/SIPA PRESS

The general exodus from Eastern Europe involved others. (Above) Turkish migrant workers and their families show their passports as they near the end of their journey from Bulgaria in the summer of 1989.

Der allgemeine Exodus aus Osteuropa erfasste auch andere. (Oben) Türkische Arbeiter und ihre Familien halten ihre Pässe hoch, als sie im Sommer 1989 aus Bulgarien ausreisen.

L'exode général hors de l'Europe de l'Est ne concerna pas les seuls Allemands de l'Est. (Ci-dessus) La fin du voyage approche pour ces travailleurs immigrés turcs et leur famille qui brandissent leur passeport pour pouvoir sortir de Bulgarie, été 1989.

SAVESCU/SIPA PRESS

Few tried to resist the whirlwind of change that was taking place in Eastern Europe. Only in Romania was there any serious attempt to beat back the people. (Above) Crowds swarm along the streets of Bucharest, December 1989.

Nur wenige versuchten, dem Sturm der Veränderung, der über Osteuropa hinwegfegte, Widerstand entgegenzusetzen. Nur in Rumänien gab es einen ernsthaften Versuch, die Volksbewegung militärisch zu unterdrücken. (Oben) Menschenmassen auf den Straßen Bukarests im Dezember 1989.

Peu nombreux furent ceux qui tentèrent de résister à la vague de changements qui déferla sur l'Europe de l'Est. Seule la Roumanie tenta de réprimer sévèrement la population. (Ci-dessus) La foule grouille dans les rues de Bucarest, décembre 1989.

The night of change… An armed member of the Romanian security forces joins the movement for liberty, Bucharest, 22–23 December 1989.

Die Nacht des Umsturzes … Ein bewaffneter Angehöriger der rumänischen Sicherheitskräfte schließt sich der Freiheitsbewegung an, Bukarest, 22./23. Dezember 1989.

La nuit du renversement … Un soldat des forces armées roumaines rejoint le mouvement pour la liberté, Bucarest, dans la nuit du 22 au 23 décembre 1989.

ANTON MANAIC/LIAISON AGENCY

(Left) Thousands gather outside the
Communist Party Central Committee
building in the centre of Bucharest,
22 December 1989. Feared and reviled,
Ceausescu lies dead (above).

(Links) Tausende versammelten sich am
22. Dezember 1989 vor dem Gebäude des
ZK der rumänischen Kommunisten im Zentrum Bukarests. (Oben) Der gefürchtete und
verhasste Ceausescu nach seiner Hinrichtung.

(À gauche) Des milliers de gens se réunirent
devant le siège du Comité central du parti
communiste dans le centre de Bucarest,
le 22 décembre 1989. Après avoir été craint
et honni, Ceausescu gît défunt (ci-dessus).

The return of Dubcek, Prague, November 1989. Twenty years after he had been expelled from the Communist Party, Alexander Dubcek left the timber yard where he had been working as a clerk, to greet crowds in the Czechoslovakian capital.

Die Rückkehr Alexander Dubceks, Prag, November 1989. 20 Jahre nach seinem Ausschluss aus der Kommunistischen Partei konnte der einstige Parteichef das Sägewerk verlassen, in dem er angestellt war. Eine jubelnde Menge empfing ihn in der tschechoslowakischen Hauptstadt.

Le retour de Dubcek, Prague, novembre 1989. Vingt ans après avoir été exclu du parti communiste, Alexandre Dubcek quitte la scierie où il travaillait comme employé de bureau, pour saluer la foule réunie dans la capitale tchécoslovaque.

The arrival of Havel, Prague, December 1989. Ten months earlier, Václav Havel (second from left) had been imprisoned for subversion. Now he had been elected President of Czechoslovakia by popular vote.

Die Ankunft Havels, Prag, Dezember 1989. Zehn Monate zuvor war Václav Havel (zweiter von links) wegen umstürzlerischer Tätigkeit inhaftiert worden. Nun wurde er vom Volk zum Präsidenten der Tschechoslowakei gewählt.

L'arrivée de Havel à Prague, décembre 1989. Emprisonné pour conduite subversive dix mois plus tôt, Vaclav Havel (deuxième depuis la gauche) venait d'être élu président de la Tchécoslovaquie suite à un vote populaire.

Euphoria on the streets of Prague. A delighted Czech
citizen celebrates the end of the Communist regime as
the 1980s draws to a dramatic end.

Begeisterung in den Straßen Prags. Ein jubelnder Tscheche
feiert am dramatischen Schlusspunkt der achtziger Jahre
den Sturz des kommunistischen Regimes.

Euphorie dans les rues de Prague. Un citoyen tchèque
enthousiaste célèbre la fin du régime communiste alors
que les années 1980 se terminent sur un coup de théâtre.

Masses on the march. Workers, students and families fill the streets of Prague during a General Strike, November 1989. The next day the Communist Prime Minister Ladislav Adamec relinquished his monopoly on power.

Eine Massendemonstration. Arbeiter, Studenten, ganze Familien füllten die Straßen Prags während des Generalstreiks im November 1989. Am folgenden Tag verzichtete der kommunistische Ministerpräsident Ladislav Adamec auf das Machtmonopol.

Manifestation de la masse. Travailleurs, étudiants et familles envahissent les rues de Prague lors d'une grève générale, novembre 1989. Le jour suivant, le Premier ministre communiste, Ladislav Adamec, renonçait au monopole du pouvoir.

'We have achieved as much as we could…' Lech Walesa leaves the meeting at which he and the Polish Government signed an agreement establishing free trade unions, Gdansk, 1 September 1980.

„Wir haben so viel erreicht, wie wir konnten …" Lech Walesa nach dem Treffen mit Vertretern der polnischen Regierung, bei dem die Vereinbarung zur Zulassung freier Gewerkschaften unterzeichnet wurde, Danzig, 1. September 1980.

« Nous avons fait tout ce que nous avons pu … » déclara Lech Walesa à la sortie d'une réunion au cours de laquelle il signa avec le gouvernement polonais un accord autorisant les syndicats libres, Gdansk, le 1ᵉʳ septembre 1980.

General Wojciech Jaruzelski (centre), Prime Minister of Poland and Communist Party leader, confers with army officers after placing his country under martial law, 13 December 1981.

Der polnische Staats- und Parteichef General Wojciech Jaruzelski (Mitte) im Gespräch mit Offizieren nach der Verhängung des Kriegsrechts über Polen am 13. Dezember 1981.

Le Général Wojciech Jaruzelski (centre), le Premier ministre polonais et dirigeant du parti communiste, en conciliabule avec des officiers de l'armée après avoir décrété la loi martiale dans tout le pays, le 13 décembre 1981.

A smiling Lech Walesa in triumphant mood
at the Gdansk Stadium, September 1983.
The following month he was awarded the
Nobel Peace Prize.

Ein lächelnder Lech Walesa als Triumphator
im Stadion von Danzig, September 1983.
Im folgenden Monat erhielt er den Friedensnobelpreis.

Un Lech Walesa souriant et triomphant
au stade de Gdansk, septembre 1983. Le
prix Nobel de la paix lui fut décerné le
mois suivant.

4. Money
Geld
L'argent

Worse than 1929. The *New York Post* headline describes the record slump on the American Stock Exchange as a 'Wall Street Bloodbath'. On 19 October 1987 the Dow Jones industrial average fell by 508 points.

Schlimmer als 1929. Die *New York Post* bezeichnete den Rekord-Kurssturz des amerikanischen Aktienmarkts in ihrer Schlagzeile als das „Blutbad an der Wall Street". Am 19. Oktober 1987 fiel der Dow-Jones-Index um 508 Punkte.

Pire que 1929. « Bain de sang à Wall Street », c'est le titre du *New York Post* pour décrire la chute spectaculaire de la bourse de New York. Le 19 octobre 1987, le taux moyen du Dow Jones chuta de 508 points.

4. Money
Geld
L'argent

When the stock markets crumpled on 19 October 1987, the Crash ruined many but overall recovery was relatively quick. There was none of the drawn-out misery that followed the Wall Street Crash of 1929. Within a few months the markets had clawed their way back to pre-Crash highs.

The Eighties were years of making money in amazing amounts. At the top of the pile of gold were the entrepreneurs, the gung-ho venture capitalists. In their wake came those equally hungry for wealth but with less imagination, the willing cohorts prepared to burn themselves out for a large slice of the action. Behind them came the hopeful, content with a fast car rather than a yacht, a comfortable house rather than a palace, a case of champagne rather than the elixir of life.

The good times kept rolling. People made money hand over fist. Never had governments been more supportive; these were glory days of ever lower taxation, ever higher profits. There was nothing that money couldn't buy except perhaps anonymity.

Als der Aktienmarkt am 19. Oktober 1987 einbrach, wurden zwar viele in den Ruin gezogen, aber der Markt erholte sich insgesamt wieder schnell. Das lang anhaltende Elend, das nach dem Zusammenbruch der Wall Street 1929 eingetreten war, blieb dieses Mal aus. Innerhalb weniger Monate erreichten die Kurse wieder das hohe Niveau, das sie vor dem Crash zu verzeichnen hatten.

In den achtziger Jahren wurde Geld in großem Stil verdient. Auf dem Gipfel des Goldhaufens thronten Unternehmer, die sich bedenkenlos auf riskante Spekulationsgeschäfte einließen. In ihrem Gefolge kamen jene, die auch nach Reichtum dürsteten, aber weniger Phantasie hatten, die willigen Kohorten, die bereit waren, sich für ihren Anteil am Kuchen voll zu verausgaben. Und dann folgten jene, die schon mit einem schnellen Auto statt einer Jacht, einem komfortablen Haus statt einem Palast und einer Kiste Champagner statt dem Elixier des Lebens zufrieden waren.

Die guten Zeiten gingen weiter. Es wurde leichtes Geld verdient. Niemals waren die Regierungen freundlicher gewesen; es herrschten die glorreichen Zeiten ständig sinkender Steuern und wachsender Profite. Alles ließ sich mit Geld kaufen, abgesehen vielleicht von Anonymität.

La chute des marchés boursiers le 19 octobre 1987 causa la ruine de beaucoup de monde, mais la reprise fut relativement rapide pour l'ensemble de l'économie. Cette crise n'engendra pas de misère durable comme cela fut le cas après le krach de Wall St reet en 1929. En quelques mois, les marchés reconquirent les sommets qu'ils avaient atteints avant la date fatidique.

Les années quatre-vingt furent l'occasion de gagner des sommes d'argent fabuleuses. En tête de liste des plus grosses fortunes figuraient les entrepreneurs, ces investisseurs en capital-risque à la fois enthousiastes et naïfs. Dans leur sillage suivaient des hommes tout aussi avides d'argent mais sans imagination, des cohortes de volontaires prêts à tout pour se faire une place au soleil. Enfin, il y avait les ambitieux plus modestes qui préféraient la voiture de sport au yacht, la jolie maison au palace et qui se contentaient d'une caisse de champagne plutôt que de l'élixir de longue vie.

L'époque était fastueuse, sans aucune ombre au tableau. Les gens gagnaient de l'argent plus qu'il n'en fallait. Les gouvernements n'avaient jamais été autant à l'écoute, favorisant les réductions d'impôts tandis que les profits ne cessaient d'augmenter. L'argent pouvait tout acheter, excepté l'anonymat.

Alternative takes on
the Market Crash.
(Left) On the same
day, a trader slumps
in his seat on
the floor of the
New York
Stock Exchange.

Verschiedene
Reaktionen auf den
Kurssturz. (Links)
An diesem Tag sackt
ein Makler der New
Yorker Börse in sich
zusammen.

Face au krach bour-
sier, deux réactions
différentes …
(À gauche) Un trader
effondré sur son
siège à la bourse de
New York le jour de
la chute des cours.

TOM SOBOLIK/BLACK STAR/COLORIFIC!

JOSEPH RODRIGUEZ/BLACK STAR/COLORIFIC!

Two days after the Crash, Freddy (a representative of the less affluent) parades outside the NY Stock Exchange. His poster sez: 'Lost money on Wall Street? Who me? I'm broke already!'

Zwei Tage später demonstriert Freddy (einer, dem es schon vorher schlecht ging) vor der New Yorker Börse. Auf seiner Papptafel heißt es: „Geld an der Wall Street verloren? Und ich? Ich bin schon längst pleite!"

Deux jours après le krach, Freddy (représentant des non-fortunés) défile devant la bourse de New York. Son affiche dit « Perdu de l'argent à Wall Street ? Et moi alors ? J'suis déjà ruiné ! »

But the show goes on. Dealers crane forward to make their bids at the London Metal Exchange as the markets rise again in 1989.

Aber die Show geht weiter. Makler der London Metal Exchange im vollen Einsatz, um ihre Gebote abzugeben, als sich die Kurse wieder erholen, 1989.

Mais le spectacle continue. Les agents de change tendent le cou pour faire leurs transactions à la bourse de Londres tandis que les marchés remontent à nouveau en 1989.

THE STOCK EXCHANGE

In the wake of Wall Street. A dealer hurries to the London Stock Exchange. Black Monday (19 October) was a bad day across the Western world.

Die Auswirkungen des Kurseinbruchs an der Wall Street. Ein Händler eilt zur Londoner Börse. Der Schwarze Montag (19. Oktober) war für die Wirtschaft der gesamten westlichen Welt ein böser Tag.

Dans le sillage du krach de Wall Street. Trader pressé d'atteindre la bourse de Londres. Le lundi noir (19 octobre) fut un mauvais jour sur tous les marchés du monde occidental.

DAVID GIBSON

French dealers rush to the Paris Bourse, 21 October 1987. On that day the Dow rose by a record 186 points, to recover almost half its original loss, but there were more falls to come.

Französische Makler spurten zur Pariser Börse, 21. Oktober 1987. An diesem Tag stieg der Dow-Jones-Index um 186 Punkte, ein Rekord, der fast die Hälfte der eingetretenen Verluste wettmachte. Es sollten aber noch neue Kurseinbrüche folgen.

Les agents de change parisiens regagnent en courant la bourse de Paris le 21 octobre 1987. Ce jour-là, le taux du Dow Jones grimpa de 186 points, chiffre record, regagnant ainsi la moitié de sa valeur initiale, mais de nouvelles chutes allaient suivre.

Summer greed. In August 1984 the British motor company Jaguar was floated on the Stock Exchange. (Above) Those who left their application for shares until the last day fight to hand in their forms.

Gier im Sommer. Im August 1984 ging die britische Autofirma Jaguar an die Börse. (Oben) Diejenigen, die bis zum letzten Tag mit dem Kauf von Aktien gewartet hatten, kämpften mit Händen und Füßen, um ihre Optionen einzureichen.

Avidité estivale. En août 1984, Jaguar, le fabricant de voitures britannique, fut lancé en bourse. (Ci-dessus) Après avoir attendu le dernier jour pour remettre leur formulaire de souscription, ces gens se battent pour le faire enregistrer avant l'expiration du délai.

Autumn greed.
Would-be share-
holders in the
Laura Ashley fashion
empire form a last
minute queue,
Farringdon Street,
London,
28 November 1985.

Gier aber auch im
Herbst. Präsumtive
Anteilseigner des
Modeimperiums
Laura Ashley stehen
Schlange, um in letz-
ter Minute Aktien zu
kaufen, Farringdon
Street, London,
28. November 1985.

Avidité automnale.
Foule de gens qui
espèrent devenir
actionnaires de
Laura Ashley,
empire de la mode,
avant l'expiration
du délai de souscrip-
tion, Farringdon
Street, Londres, le
28 novembre 1985.

MARK RICHARDS/COLORIFIC!

Lending a Presidential hand – let's hope he washed them first.
President George Bush visits former industrial workers who have
retrained to work in a branch of Domino's Pizza.

Der Präsident packt selber mit an – hoffentlich hat er sich vorher die
Hände gewaschen. George Bush besucht ehemalige Industriearbeiter
bei einer Umschulungsmaßnahme. Sie sollen in Zukunft für Domino's
Pizza arbeiten.

Coup de main présidentiel, espérons qu'elles soient propres … Visite
du président George Bush dans un restaurant de Domino's Pizza qui a
permis à d'anciens ouvriers d'usine de retrouver un emploi.

Bending a Prime Ministerial ear. Margaret Thatcher (left) visits the Pattersons at their newly acquired home in Harold Hill, Essex. They were the 12,000th family to buy their home from the GLC (courtesy of State sell-offs).

Die Premierministerin zu Gast. Margaret Thatcher (links) besucht die Pattersons in deren neu erworbenem Haus in Harold Hill, Essex. Sie waren die zwölftausendste Familie, die ihr Haus im Rahmen von Verkäufen von Häusern aus öffentlichem Besitz vom Greater London Council erwarben.

Premier Ministre à l'écoute. Margaret Thatcher (à gauche) rend visite aux Patterson, propriétaires de leur logement de fraîche date, Harold Hill, Essex. Ils étaient la 12 000ᵉ famille à racheter leur appartement aux offices HLM du Greater London Council (avec la bénédiction de l'État).

The new tycoons. (Left) Bill Gates, founder of the Microsoft Corporation, 1985. He was well on his way to becoming the richest man in the world.

Die neuen Tycoone. (Links) Bill Gates, Gründer der Microsoft Corporation, 1985. Er war schon dabei, der reichste Mann der Welt zu werden.

Les nouveaux magnats. (À gauche) Bill Gates, fondateur de Microsoft Corporation, 1985. Il n'allait pas tarder à devenir l'homme le plus riche du monde.

(Right) Steve Jobs, co-founder of Apple Computers, and later head of Pixar Studios, makers of *Toy Story*.

(Rechts) Steve Jobs, Mitbegründer von Apple Computers und später Leiter der Pixar Studios, die *Toy Story* produzierten.

(À droite) Steve Jobs, cofondateur de Apple Computers, et futur directeur des Studios Pixar, créateurs de *Toy Story*.

TERENCE SPENCER/COLORIFIC!

Happy landings. Richard Branson plays in the bath, promoting Virgin
Atlantic Airways. The company was founded in 1984 after Branson
had been forced to sell his record empire.

Glückliche Landung. Richard Branson plantscht in der Badewanne,
um für Virgin Atlantic Airways zu werben. Die Firma wurde 1984
gegründet, nachdem Branson gezwungen worden war, sein Platten-
imperium zu verkaufen.

Atterrissage réussi. Richard Branson joue dans le bain et fait la publicité de Virgin Atlantic Airways. La compagnie fut fondée par Branson
en 1984 après qu'il eut été obligé de vendre son empire du disque.

Hullo, John, got a new motor…? John DeLorean proudly displays a picture of his gull-winged, stainless steel sports car. Despite massive publicity and enormous subsidies from the British Government, the car was a commercial failure.

Hullo, John, got a new motor … ? John DeLorean präsentiert stolz ein Foto seines neuen windschnittigen Sportwagens mit Karosserie aus rostfreiem Stahl. Obwohl die Werbetrommel mächtig gerührt wurde und die britische Regierung nicht mit Subventionen sparte, blieb der wirtschaftliche Erfolg des neuen Modells aus.

Hullo, John, got a new motor … ? » John DeLorean fier de sa voiture de sport à portes papillon et en acier inoxydable. Malgré une énorme campagne de publicité et d'importantes aides attribuées par le gouvernement britannique, la voiture fut un échec commercial.

MARIO RUIZ/COLORIFIC!

Playing the Trump card… Donald and Ivana Trump pose in the Ruby Room of their luxury yacht the *Trump Princess*, 7 April 1988. Three months later he acquired the *Nabila*, the largest yacht in the world.

Die Trumps trumpfen auf … Donald und Ivana Trump posieren im Rubinzimmer ihrer Luxusjacht *Trump Princess,* 7. April 1988. Drei Monate später kaufte Trump die *Nabila,* die größte Jacht der Welt.

Jouer la carte Trump. Donald et Ivana Trump posent dans la chambre Ruby de leur yacht de luxe, le *Trump Princess,* le 7 avril 1988. Trois mois plus tard, Donald Trump acheta le *Nabila,* le plus grand yacht du monde.

Big hair day… Peter Stringfellow, owner of the eponymous London club at ease with champagne and underdressed blondes. His consumption of both was conspicious in the Eighties.

Haarige Zeiten … Peter Stringfellow, der Eigentümer des gleichnamigen Londoner Clubs, vergnügt sich mit Champagner und leicht bekleideten Blondinen. In beider Hinsicht war er in den achtziger Jahren für seinen gewaltigen Konsum berühmt.

La belle vie … Peter Stringfellow, propriétaire du club londonien du même nom, à l'aise avec une coupe de champagne et quelques blondes légèrement vêtues. Sa consommation des deux attira beaucoup l'attention sur lui dans les années 1980.

LAURENCE CENDROWICZ/COLORIFIC!

'Only the little people pay taxes…' Leona Helmsley displays hubris as she poses beside a portrait of her husband, June 1989. Her hotel empire ran into difficulties when she was accused of tax evasion on a grand scale.

„Nur die kleinen Leute zahlen Steuern …" Leona Helmsley posiert voller Hybris neben einem Porträt ihres Gatten, Juni 1989. Ihr Hotelimperium kam in Schwierigkeiten, als sie wegen in großem Maßstab verübter Steuerhinterziehung angeklagt wurde.

« Il n'y a que les petites gens pour payer des impôts … » Leona Helmsley affiche son orgueil démesuré en posant devant un portrait de son mari, juin 1989. Son empire hôtelier connut des difficultés dès lors qu'elle fut accusée d'évasion fiscale à grande échelle.

TOM IVES/BLACK STAR/COLORIFIC!

Wrapped up against the cold. A woman attempts to keep herself warm in a bus shelter at Phoenix, Arizona, December 1983. The general increase in wealth was accompanied by a huge rise in the number of people living in poverty.

Eingemummt gegen die Kälte. Eine Frau versucht, sich an einer Bushaltestelle in Phoenix, Arizona, notdürftig warm zu halten, Dezember 1983. Trotz der allgemeinen Zunahme des Reichtums stieg die Zahl der Menschen, die in Armut lebten, stark an.

Enveloppée pour se protéger du froid. Une femme tente de se réchauffer sous un abri de bus à Phoenix, Arizona, décembre 1983. L'augmentation générale des richesses fut accompagnée d'une hausse du nombre de personnes vivant dans la pauvreté.

ROGER CHARITY/COLORIFIC!

Cushioned against discomfort. Joan Collins relaxes on a sofa newly delivered from Heal's, the London furniture store. This one looked better without the plastic wrapping.

Gut gepolstert. Joan Collins entspannt sich auf dem neu gelieferten Sofa des Londoner Möbelhauses Heal's. Ohne Plastikverpackung sähe es wohl besser aus.

Protégée contre les risques d'inconfort. Instant de détente pour Joan Collins, allongée sur un canapé fraîchement livré par Heal's, le célèbre magasin de meubles de Londres. Il sera plus chic une fois débarrassé de la protection en plastique.

5. Entertainment
Unterhaltung
Les divertissements

Lauren Hutton and Richard Gere make an unsuccessful attempt to avoid the
attention of the press at the preview of their 1980 film *American Gigolo*, directed
by Paul Schrader. Christopher Reeve had previously rejected Gere's role.

Lauren Hutton und Richard Gere versuchen erfolglos, der Aufmerksamkeit der
Fotografen bei der Voraufführung ihres Films *Ein Mann für gewisse Stunden*
(Regie: Paul Schrader) zu entgehen, 1980. Christopher Reeve hatte zuvor Geres
Rolle abgelehnt.

Lauren Hutton et Richard Gere font tout pour ne pas attirer l'attention de
la presse lors de la projection de leur film *American Gigolo,* dirigé par Paul
Schrader, en 1980. Christopher Reeve avait décliné le rôle de Gere.

5. Entertainment
Unterhaltung
Les divertissements

Times were good for the stars. Television audiences reached an all-time peak for the on-going dramas of the TV soaps *Dallas* and *Dynasty*. Film budgets reached their highest levels of all time – *Batman* cost $50 million, *Who Framed Roger Rabbit?* held the record for a while at $70 million. The returns on such massive capital outlays made it all worthwhile – *ET* alone grossed $228 million.

Much of the credit for this renewed vigour and profitability went to Steven Spielberg. Almost single-handedly he revived the notion of family outings to the cinema, with films that brought back memories of the golden days of the 1940s and early 1950s. It was a considerable achievement, for video recorders were to be found in more and more homes and the age of the couch potato was looming.

The Eighties also saw a continuation in the rise of violence on TV and cinema screen. Arnie Schwarzenegger splattered his enemies against innumerable walls; in *Die Hard* Bruce Willis did more damage to LA than the earthquake of October 1987. George Lucas completed his *Star Wars* trilogy, and science fiction became the most popular movie genre.

Es waren gute Zeiten für Stars. Die Zuschauerzahlen des Fernsehens stiegen mit den Endlos-Serien *Dallas* und *Denver Clan* auf nie wieder erreichte Rekordhöhen. Die Filmbudgets waren ebenfalls so groß wie noch nie – *Batman* kostete 50 Millionen Dollar, *Falsches Spiel mit Roger Rabbit* hielt mit 70 Millionen Dollar eine Zeit lang den Rekord. Die Gewinne machten diese riesigen Kapitalinvestitionen zu einem profitablen Geschäft – allein *E. T.* spielte 228 Millionen Dollar ein.

Die wiedergewonnene Stärke und Profitabilität des Kinos war zu einem großen Teil Steven Spielberg zu danken. Fast allein machte er den Familienausflug ins Kino wieder populär, mit Filmen, die Erinnerungen an die goldenen Tage der vierziger und frühen fünfziger Jahre weckten. Das war eine umso erstaunlichere Leistung, als die Video-rekorder in immer mehr Haushalte gelangten und das Zeitalter des Dauerglotzens anbrach.

In den achtziger Jahren setzte sich die Zunahme von Gewaltszenen in Film und Fernsehen weiter fort. Arnold Schwarzenegger schmetterte seine Feinde gegen unzählige Wände; in *Stirb Langsam* verwüstete Bruce Willis Los Angeles stärker als das Erdbeben vom Oktober 1987. George Lucas komplettierte seine *Krieg der Sterne*-Trilogie; Science-fiction wurde zum beliebtesten Filmgenre.

Ce fut une belle époque pour les stars. La télévision battit tous les records d'audience avec *Dallas* et *Dynasty,* deux feuilletons riches en rebondissements dramatiques. Les budgets de film furent plus élevés que jamais. *Batman* coûta 50 millions de dollars. *Qui a tué Roger Rabbit ?* détint le record absolu pendant quelque temps avec un budget de 70 millions de dollars. Les profits tirés de ces dépenses faramineuses valaient la peine de prendre des risques. Le film d'*E.T.* généra 228 millions de dollars de recettes.

Si le cinéma recouvra une telle santé et renoua avec les bénéfices, c'est surtout grâce à Steven Spielberg. C'est lui seul ou presque qui sut raviver le plaisir des sorties en famille au cinéma en produisant des films qui rappelaient l'âge d'or des années quarante et du début années cinquante. Ce fut une réussite immense car de plus en plus de foyers étaient pourvus de magnétoscopes et l'ère des consommateurs passifs de télévision approchait.

Les années quatre-vingt furent également une décennie durant laquelle la violence augmenta progressivement sur les écrans de télévision et de cinéma. Arnold Schwarzen-egger passait son temps à écraser ses ennemis contre les murs tandis que Bruce Willis dans *Die Hard* causait plus de ravages dans Los Angeles que le tremblement de terre d'octobre 1987. Enfin, George Lucas termina sa trilogie, *La Guerre des étoiles,* et la science-fiction devint le genre cinématographique le plus populaire.

Dan Aykroyd (left)
and John Belushi hit
the road after the
success of John
Landis's 1980 cult
movie *The Blues
Brothers*.

Dan Aykroyd (links)
und John Belushi
hauen nach dem
Erfolg von John
Landis' Kultfilm
Blues Brothers
(1980) mächtig auf
den Putz.

Dan Aykroyd
(à gauche) et John
Belushi sur la route
après le succès du
film culte de 1980,
The Blues Brothers,
réalisé par John
Landis.

Danny de Vito and Rhea Perlman (Carla from *Cheers*) present themselves as that rare phenomenon, a happy Hollywood couple, 1983.

Danny de Vito und Rhea Perlman (die Carla aus *Cheers*) präsentieren sich als die Ausnahme-erscheinung eines glücklichen Holly-wood-Ehepaars, 1983.

Danny de Vito et Rhea Perlman (Carla dans *Cheers*) forment un couple heureux, ce qui est un phénomène rare à Hollywood, 1983.

Martin Scorsese and Rosanna Arquette on the set of *New York Stories*, 1989. The film was a 'three-course meal' – three tales directed by three directors, Scorsese, Francis Ford Coppola and Woody Allen. It failed.

Martin Scorsese und Rosanna Arquette während der Arbeit an *New Yorker Geschichten*, 1989. Der Film war ein „Menü mit drei Gängen" – drei Geschichten, die von drei Regisseuren, Scorsese, Francis Ford Coppola und Woody Allen, verfilmt wurden. Ein Kassenerfolg wurde er nicht.

Martin Scorcese et Rosanna Arquette sur le tournage de *New York Stories*, 1989. Le film se voulait comme un menu composé de trois plats, c'est-à-dire trois histoires dirigées par trois metteurs en scène différents, Scorsese, Francis Ford Coppola et Woody Allen. Ce fut un échec.

JEFFREY AARONSON/COLORIFIC!

Before it fell apart… Jack Nicholson and Anjelica Huston gaze fondly at each other in Gordon's Rest, Aspen, Colorado. In the 1980s Aspen was home to many movie stars, including Nicholson, Goldie Hawn and Cher.

Bevor es auseinander ging … Jack Nicholson und Anjelica Huston schmachten sich gegenseitig an, Gordon's Rest, Aspen, Colorado. In den achtziger Jahren lebten viele Filmstars in Aspen, darunter Nicholson, Goldie Hawn und Cher.

Avant la rupture … Jack Nicholson et Anjelica Huston se regardent tendrement au Gordon's Rest à Aspen dans le Colorado. Dans les années 1980, Aspen fut fréquenté par de nombreuses vedettes du cinéma, dont Nicholson, Goldie Hawn et Cher.

MOSHE SHAI/SHOOTING STAR/COLORIFIC!

Chilling out in the Middle East. After a hectic film schedule in the late 1970s (*Taxi Driver*, *Raging Bull* and *New York, New York*) Robert de Niro takes time off to smoke a little hash through a bong.

Entspannung im Nahen Osten. Nach hektischen Dreharbeiten in den späten siebziger Jahren *(Taxi Driver, Wie ein wilder Stier* und *New York, New York)* gönnt sich Robert de Niro einen Zug Hasch aus der Wasserpfeife.

Frissons au Moyen-Orient. Après avoir tourné film sur film à la fin des années 1970 *(Taxi Driver, Raging Bull* et *New York, New York)*, Robert de Niro prend du bon temps et se détend en fumant un peu de hachisch au narguilé.

Alan Alda (left) enjoys Warren Beatty's moment of glory as the latter holds his Director's Guild of America Award for *Reds*, 13 March 1982.

Alan Alda (links) freut sich mit Warren Beatty, als dieser für *Reds* den Preis der Director's Guild of America erhält, 13. März 1982.

Alan Alda (à gauche) est aussi heureux que Warren Beatty qui vient de recevoir l'oscar du meilleur réalisateur pour son film *Reds*, 13 mars 1982.

BOB SCOTT/FOTOS INTERNATIONAL/HULTON|ARCHIVE

The price of fame. Sean Penn (left) and an almost obscured Madonna run the gauntlet of Hollywood photographers, 1985. It was the year of Madonna's first film, *Desperately Seeking Susan*.

Der Preis des Ruhms. Sean Penn (links) und die fast verdeckte Madonna beim Spießrutenlauf durch die Schar der Hollywood-Fotografen, 1985. In diesem Jahr kam Madonnas erster Film heraus, *Susan … verzweifelt gesucht*.

Le prix de la gloire. Sean Penn (à gauche) et une Madonna presque invisible endurent les flashes des photographes de Hollywood, 1985. Ce fut l'année de la sortie du premier film de Madonna, *Recherche Susan désespérément*.

COLORIFIC!

An actor comes face to face with reality. Nastassja Kinski gets some tips from a real bear on the set of *The Hotel New Hampshire*, 1984. Kinski played the part of Susie the bear in the movie.

Die Schöne und das Tier. Nastassja Kinski bekommt bei den Dreharbeiten zu *Hotel New Hampshire*, 1984, ein Küsschen von einem echten Bären. Kinski spielte damals die Rolle von Susie, der Bärin.

Quand un acteur est confronté à la réalité. Nastassja Kinski reçoit des conseils d'un vrai ours sur le tournage du film *The Hotel New Hampshire*, dans lequel elle joue le rôle de Susie l'ours, 1984.

MAURO CARRARO/COLORIFIC!

Christopher Lambert sits with his on-screen adoptive mother on the set of Hugh Hudson's 1984 movie *Greystoke: The Legend of Tarzan, Lord of the Apes*. Some critics unkindly suggested that the apes came closer to Oscar-winning performances.

Christopher Lambert neben der Darstellerin, die in Hugh Hudsons *Greystoke – Die Legende von Tarzan, Herr der Affen* (1984), seine Adoptivmutter spielte. Misslaunige Kritiker nörgelten, das schauspielerische Können der Affen sei noch Oscar-verdächtiger als Lamberts.

Christophe Lambert assis en compagnie de sa mère adoptive dans *Greystoke : La légende de Tarzan*, le film de Hugh Hudson, 1984. Des critiques malveillants firent remarquer que les singes auraient bien mérité un oscar du meilleur acteur.

CAVALIER/SHOOTING STAR/COLORIFIC!

David Hasselhoff poses beside the star of the show, a talking car, in the TV series *Knight Rider*. For Hasselhoff, ahead lay *Baywatch* and even greater fame. For the car, it was the scrap heap. That's showbiz!

David Hasselhoff posiert neben dem wahren Star der Sendung, dem sprechenden Auto der Fernsehserie *Knight Rider*. Auf Hasselhoff warteten *Baywatch* und noch größerer Ruhm. Auf das Auto wartete der Schrottplatz. So ist es nun einmal im Showgeschäft.

David Hasselhoff pose devant le personnage principal, une voiture parlante, de la série télévisée intitulée *Knight Rider*. Hasselhoff allait devenir plus célèbre encore, notamment avec *Baywatch*. Quant à la voiture, elle n'avait pour futur que la casse. C'est ça le show-biz !

Tom Selleck and his moustache try to steal the thunder from their co-star, the red Ferrari, in the TV series *Magnum*.

Tom Selleck und sein Schnauzbart brauchen sich nicht hinter dem Co-Star, dem roten Ferrari aus der Fernsehserie *Magnum* zu verstecken.

Tom Selleck et sa moustache tentent de voler la vedette à l'autre star de la série télévisée *Magnum*, la fameuse Ferrari rouge.

Woody Allen makes his weekly visit to Michael's Pub, Manhattan, to wail with the New Orleans Funeral and Ragtime Orchestra, 1980.

Woody Allen bei seinem wöchentlichen Gastspiel in Michael's Pub, wo er mit dem New Orleans Funeral and Ragtime Orchestra jazzt, 1980.

Woody Allen à la clarinette, lors de son rendez-vous hebdomadaire au Michael's Pub à Manhattan pour jouer avec le New Orleans Funeral and Ragtime Orchestra, 1980.

BERNARD GOTFRYD/COLORIFIC!

Eddie Murphy takes time out from *Trading Places* wearing a white suit to do his famous impression of the young Alec Guinness at Bentley's Disco.

Eddie Murphy nutzt eine Drehpause von *Die Glücksritter*, um im weißen Anzug in Bentley's Disco seine Imitation des jungen Alec Guinness vorzuführen.

Moment de détente pour Eddie Murphy, après *Trading Places*, qui fait son fameux numéro en costume blanc : Alec Guinness en discothèque chez Bentley's.

Giving the game away… How *did* they make Henry Thomas fly for *ET: The Extra Terrestrial*, Hollywood, 1982? The technique was called Blue Screen.

Der Trick wird preisgegeben … Wie konnte Henry Thomas in *E. T. – Der Außerirdische* nur fliegen, Hollywood, 1982? Das Blaustanzverfahren machte es möglich.

Révéler le truc de magie … Comment ont-ils réussi à faire voler Henry Thomas dans *E.T. l'extra-terrestre,* à Hollywood en 1982 ? En utilisant la technique dite du « Blue Screen ».

ET's creator Steven Spielberg lines up another shot for his 1980 blockbuster *Indiana Jones and the Temple of Doom*. It was a highly profitable time for the *Wunderkind*. Just as well: his divorce cost him $100 million.

Steven Spielberg, der Schöpfer von *E. T.*, denkt über eine neue Einstellung seines Knüllers *Indiana Jones und der Tempel des Todes* nach, 1980. In jenen Tagen klingelte die Kasse des Wunderkinds. Das war auch besser so, denn seine Scheidung kostete ihn 100 Millionen Dollar.

Steven Spielberg, le créateur de *E.T.*, enregistre un nouveau succès phénoménal en 1980 avec *Indiana Jones et le temple maudit*. L'enfant prodige du cinéma gagna énormément d'argent pendant cette époque. Tant mieux car son divorce lui coûta 100 millions de dollars.

After a string of films for TV in the early 1980s, the British director Mike Leigh made his cinema debut in 1988 with *High Hopes*.

Nach einer Reihe von Fernsehfilmen, die er in den frühen achtziger Jahren gedreht hatte, feierte der britische Regisseur Mike Leigh 1988 sein Kinodebüt mit *High Hopes*.

Après avoir réalisé une série de téléfilms au début des années 1980, le réalisateur britannique Mike Leigh fit ses débuts au cinéma en 1988 avec *High Hopes*.

JOE McNALLY/COLORIFIC!

Milos Forman relaxes at home in Danbury, Connecticut, November 1984. It was the year in which his film version of Peter Shaffer's play *Amadeus* won Oscars for Best Film, Best Director (himself) and Best Actor (F. Murray Abraham).

Milos Forman entspannt sich in seinem Haus in Danbury, Connecticut, November 1984. In diesem Jahr gewann seine Verfilmung von Peter Shaffers *Amadeus* die Oscars für den besten Film, die beste Regie (Forman selbst) und den besten Schauspieler (F. Murray Abraham).

Milos Forman se repose dans sa maison de Danbury, Connecticut, novembre 1984. Ce fut l'année où son adaptation cinématographique de la pièce de Peter Shaffer, *Amadeus,* remporta les oscars du meilleur film, du meilleur réalisateur (lui) et du meilleur acteur (F. Murray Abraham).

The paper headline says 'How to make your wimp more macho'. The mug says 'Good @*!#@* morning'. Roseanne Barr just smiles.

Die Zeitungs-schlagzeile lautet: „Wie bringen Sie ihren Jammerlappen auf Vordermann?" Auf dem Becher steht: „Guten @*!#@* Morgen". Roseanne Barr strahlt.

Le titre du journal propose de « trans-former une mau-viette de mari en un mec plus macho », la tasse de café affiche un « Good @*!#@* morning » et Roseanne Barr rigole, c'est tout.

Student Brooke Shields takes part in a stage production at Princeton University in the mid-1980s. She already had a considerable movie career behind her, having made her debut as a child.

Brooke Shields als Studentin bei einer Aufführung Mitte der achtziger Jahre an der Universität Princeton. Da hatte sie bereits eine beachtliche Filmkarriere hinter sich: Schon als Kind hatte sie vor der Kamera gestanden.

L'étudiante Brooke Shields fait partie d'un spectacle monté à l'université de Princeton au milieu des années 1980. Elle avait déjà derrière elle une longue carrière de cinéma puisqu'elle avait débuté alors qu'elle était une enfant.

SASHA STALLONE/VISAGES/COLORIFIC!

No gain (and possibly no career) without pain. Sylvester Stallone and son work out on the lawn of their Hollywood home, 1981. Ahead lay more *Rocky* films and the bullet-riddled *First Blood*.

Ohne Schweiß kein Preis (und vielleicht auch keine Karriere). Sylvester Stallone und Sohn bei der Trainingsarbeit auf dem Rasen vor ihrem Haus in Hollywood, 1981. Vor ihm lagen weitere *Rocky*-Folgen und der Kugelhagel von *Rambo – der Auftrag*.

Pas de profit (et probablement pas de carrière) sans souffrir un peu. Sylvester Stallone et son fils au travail sur la pelouse de leur demeure hollywoodienne, 1981. Au programme de tournage, il y avait quelques *Rocky* et le sanglant *Rambo*.

COLORIFIC!

Under the bashful eye of her fitness expert, Joan Collins goes through her regime at her private gym. These were the glory years of the TV series *Dynasty*, which gained audiences world-wide.

Der Trainer schaut verschämt, während Joan Collins ihr Programm in ihrem privaten Fitnessstudio durchzieht. Es waren die besten Jahre der Fernsehserie *Denver Clan*, die weltweit zum Erfolg wurde.

Sous l'œil intimidé de son professeur de fitness, Joan Collins exécute son programme sportif dans sa salle de gym privée. C'était à l'époque des glorieuses années de *Dynasty*, la série télévisée au succès planétaire.

YORAM KAHANA/SHOOTING STAR/COLORIFIC!

British actor Roger Moore relaxes in the comfort of a luxury limo. In the 1980s Moore gave up his Beretta, his exploding fountain pen, his catapulting wristwatch, and handed over the role of 007 to Timothy Dalton.

Der britische Schauspieler Roger Moore entspannt sich in einer Luxuslimousine. In den achtziger Jahren gab Moore seine Beretta, seinen explodierenden Füllfederhalter und die Armbanduhr mit abschießbarer Leine zurück. Die Rolle von James Bond übernahm Timothy Dalton.

Moment de détente pour l'acteur britannique Roger Moore, confortablement assis dans une limousine de luxe. Dans les années 1980, Moore renonça à son Beretta, à sa plume à encre explosive et à son bracelet-montre catapultant pour confier le rôle de 007 à Timothy Dalton.

Dudley Moore, another British actor, raises glass and umbrella to wealth and comfort as he poses beside a gleaming Bentley in 1981, the year in which he starred with John Gielgud in the comedy *Arthur*.

Dudley Moore, auch er ein britischer Schauspieler, hebt das Glas und den Schirm auf Wohlstand und Komfort. So posierte er 1981 neben einem schimmernden Bentley. Im gleichen Jahr spielte er neben John Gielgud in der Komödie *Arthur*.

Dudley Moore, un autre acteur britannique, pose devant une Bentley étincelante et porte un toast sous la pluie à la belle vie, 1981. Cette année-là, il joua aux côtés de John Gielguld dans *Arthur,* une comédie.

Hot shot. Charlie Sheen, Brat Packer personified, recovers from forearm decoration in a tattoo parlour.

Ein heißer Schuss. Charlie Sheen, der personifizierte böse Bube, erholt sich in einem Tattoo-Laden von der schmerzhaften Prozedur an seinem Unterarm.

Très sexy. Charlie Sheen, une des figures montantes du cinéma, se remet d'un tatouage sur l'avant-bras dans la salle d'attente.

Cruise control. Tom Cruise, Brat Pack escapee and star of the 1986 action movie *Top Gun*.

Tom Cruise, kein böser Bube mehr. Star des Actionfilms *Top Gun*, 1986.

Tom Cruise, une autre star montante, vedette du film d'action *Top Gun*, sorti en 1986.

He-man and Her-man. (Opposite) Arnold Schwarzen-egger in Conan the Barbarian mode. (Right) Paul Reubens on the set of *Pee-Wee's Playhouse*, September 1986.

He-Man und Her-man. (Gegenüberlie-gende Seite) Arnold Schwarzenegger in Conan-der-Barbar-Pose. (Rechts) Paul Reubens in den Kulissen von *Pee-Wee's Playhouse*, September 1986.

Monsieur Muscles et Gringalet. (Ci-contre) Arnold Schwarzenegger en Conan le Barbare. (À droite) Paul Reubens sur le tournage du film *Pee-Wee's Playhouse*, septembre 1986.

DOUG MENUEZ/COLORIFIC!

Doris Day and Rock Hudson. A few weeks before his death from AIDS in October 1985, Hudson spoke of his illness in a courageous attempt to draw attention to the seriousness of the AIDS epidemic.

Doris Day und Rock Hudson, einige Wochen, bevor der Schauspieler im Oktober 1985 an Aids starb. Mutig ging Hudson mit seiner Krankheit an die Öffentlichkeit, um auf die ernsten Gefahren von Aids aufmerksam zu machen.

Doris Day et Rock Hudson. Quelques semaines avant de mourir du sida en octobre 1985, Hudson parla ouvertement de sa maladie, une courageuse initiative pour attirer l'attention du public sur la gravité du sida.

Elizabeth Taylor at an AIDS Conference in the late 1980s. Throughout the 1980s, Taylor gave her support to the campaign against AIDS.

Elizabeth Taylor bei einer Aids-Konferenz Ende der achtziger Jahre. In den gesamten achtziger Jahren unterstützte die Schauspielerin den Kampf gegen Aids.

Elizabeth Taylor lors d'une conférence sur le sida à la fin des années 1980. Taylor apporta son soutien à la campagne contre le sida durant toute la décennie.

DENNIS BRACK/BLACK STAR/COLORIFIC!

6. The Arts
Die Künste
Les arts

Surrounded by his intricate graffiti-style designs, the American artist Keith Haring stares into the camera. One of his most celebrated works was a series of comical stick figures that decorated subway stations in New York. Haring died of AIDS in 1990.

Inmitten seiner komplexen Graffiti-artigen Zeichenwelt blickt der amerikanische Künstler Keith Haring in die Kamera. Sehr berühmt wurden seine komischen Strichmännchen in New Yorker U-Bahn-Stationen. Haring starb 1990 an Aids.

Au milieu de ses dessins complexes exécutés comme des graffitis, l'artiste américain Keith Haring fixe la caméra. L'une de ses œuvres les plus célèbres est la série de silhouettes comiques qui décorent les stations de métro de New York. Haring mourut du sida en 1990.

6. The Arts
Die Künste
Les arts

European artists and art brokers cast their nets widely in the 1980s, turning for inspiration and profit to the art of Africa, Asia and South America. It was the age of multi-ethnic influence, a time when artists in New York, Paris and London borrowed from other, older civilisations. It was the age of multimedia presentation, exhibitions that featured video displays or linked works of art to gently humming computers. And it was the age of corporate sponsorship – after all, every new atrium needed its sculpted centre-piece.

The literary world was much enlivened by the death threat that hung over Salman Rushdie following the publication of *The Satanic Verses* in 1988. The book was banned and burned in India, and in Iran the Ayatollah Khomeini issued a *fatwa* against Rushdie the following year. A clutch of playwrights kept the straight theatre in good heart – David Mamet, Peter Shaffer, David Hare, Sam Shepard, Arthur Miller and many more. The stage musical plundered the history and geography syllabus for ever more unlikely subjects for a hit.

Die europäischen Künstler und Kunsthändler warfen ihre Netze in den achtziger Jahren weit aus und wandten sich auf der Suche nach Inspirationen und Profiten der Kunst Afrikas, Asiens und Südamerikas zu. Es war eine Zeit multikultureller Einflüsse, als Künstler in New York, Paris oder London Anregungen aus anderen, älteren Kulturen entlehnten. Es war eine Zeit der Multimedia-Schauen, wo Ausstellungen Videokunst oder mit leise summenden Computern verbundene Kunstwerke zeigten. Und es war eine Zeit, wo Firmen Kunst förderten – schließlich brauchte der Innenhof jedes neuen Firmensitzes eine Skulptur als Blickfang.

Die literarische Welt erregte die Todesdrohung, unter der Salman Rushdie nach der Veröffentlichung der *Satanischen Verse* (1988) lebte. In Indien wurde das Buch verboten und verbrannt, im Iran verkündete Ayatollah Khomeini im folgenden Jahr eine Fatwa gegen den Schriftsteller. Eine Reihe von Bühnenautoren wie David Mamet, Peter Shaffer, David Hare, Sam Shepard oder Arthur Miller hielten das Sprechtheater in Gang. Auf der Suche nach Themen für ein erfolgreiches Musical wurden immer abgelegenere historische und geographische Gebiete durchstöbert.

Durant les années quatre-vingt, les artistes et marchands d'art européens élargirent leurs horizons en se tournant vers les arts africain, asiatique et sud-américain pour renouveler leur inspiration et fortune. Les influences devinrent multi-ethniques, les artistes de New York, de Paris et de Londres empruntant à d'autres civilisations, plus anciennes. Ce fut l'époque du multimédia, des expositions qui mettaient en scène des magnétoscopes et reliaient les œuvres d'art à des ordinateurs ronronnants en toute quiétude. Ce fut aussi l'époque du mécénat d'entreprise – il fallait désormais une sculpture dans le hall d'entrée de chaque nouvelle entreprise.

Le monde littéraire retrouva une actualité soudaine avec la menace de mort qui s'abattit sur Salman Rushdie après la publication des *Versets sataniques* en 1988. Le livre fut censuré et brûlé en Inde. L'année suivante, en Iran, l'ayatollah Khomeiny prononça une fatwa à l'encontre de Rushdie. Au théâtre, un petit groupe de dramaturges s'employaient à maintenir la scène bien vivante, comme David Mamet, Peter Shaffer, David Hare, Sam Shepard, Arthur Miller et d'autres encore. Du côté de la comédie musicale, il semblait que les programmes d'histoire et de géographie étaient passés au crible pour trouver des sujets toujours plus inattendus et susceptibles d'être de grands succès.

Gilbert Proesch and
George Passmore
(aka Gilbert and
George) pose in
front of yet another
self-made bid for
immortality,
July 1987.

Gilbert Proesch und
George Passmore
(auch bekannt als
Gilbert und George)
posieren vor einem
neuen unsterblichen
Meisterwerk,
Juli 1987.

Gilbert Proesch et
George Passmore
(alias Gilbert et
George) posent
devant leur auto-
portrait, encore un
défi à l'immortalité,
juillet 1987.

Art hit the streets and the walls as never before in the 1980s, bursting out of the studio and the gallery to decorate buses, trains, sheds, in fact any large flat surface. (Above) An artistic use of condoms for an AIDS billboard, August 1989.

Die Künste gingen in den achtziger Jahren in nie gekanntem Ausmaß auf die Straße. Die Kunst brach aus den Ateliers und Galerien aus und widmete sich Autobussen, Zügen, Lagerräumen, praktisch allen verfügbaren großen Flächen. (Oben) Kondome kommen auf einer Aids-Warntafel zu künstlerischem Einsatz, August 1989.

Dans les années 1980, l'art s'impose dans la rue et sur les murs comme jamais auparavant, explosant hors des ateliers et des galeries pour décorer les bus, les trains, les abris, à vrai dire n'importe quelle surface plate. (Ci-dessus) Usage artistique de préservatifs pour illustrer un panneau de sida, août 1989.

Graffiti reached the level of high art, with a discernible sense of style and a riotously rich use of colour. At its best, it brought at least momentary joy to dingy neighbourhoods. (Above) Old-school graffiti in Newcastle, 1985.

Graffiti wurden zur schönen Kunst, das Formgefühl wuchs, die Palette war reichhaltig und bunt. Auf jeden Fall brachte die Graffitikunst zumindest kurze Freude in trostlose Viertel. (Oben) Graffiti alten Stils in Newcastle, 1985.

Le graffiti est élevé au rang de grand art, avec un sens certain du style et un usage des couleurs à la fois riche et conflictuel. Dans le meilleur des cas, il sut dégager une sorte de joie éphémère dans les quartiers délabrés. (Ci-dessus) Graffiti de la vieille école à Newcastle, 1985.

M GODDARD/COLORIFIC!

David Hockney, doyen of modern British painters, continued to spend most of his time in California throughout the 1980s. He turned increasingly to photography as an art form, hence the camera.

David Hockney, der Doyen der modernen britischen Maler, lebte auch in den achtziger Jahren die meiste Zeit in Kalifornien. Er wandte sich zunehmend der Fotografie als künstlerischer Ausdrucksform zu, daher die Kamera.

David Hockney, doyen des peintres britanniques modernes, vécut principalement en Californie durant les années 1980. Hockney s'intéressa de plus en plus à la photographie comme forme d'art, d'où ce cliché du peintre avec un appareil photo.

The graffiti artist, Jean-Michel Basquiat, New York City, 1980. Basquiat died from a heroin overdose in 1988 at the age of 27.

Der Graffiti-Künstler Jean-Michel Basquiat, New York City, 1980. Basquiat starb 1988 im Alter von 27 Jahren an einer Überdosis Heroin.

L'artiste, Jean-Michel Basquiat, à New York en 1980. Basquiat mourut d'une overdose d'héroïne en 1988, à l'âge de 27 ans.

NAOKI OKAMOTO/BLACK STAR/COLORIFIC!

MARK CAFFERTY/BLACK STAR/COLORIFIC!

King of Kool and Prince of Pop. Jazz musician Miles Davis (left) and Andy Warhol, 16 February 1987. Exactly one week later, Warhol died after a gall bladder operation.

Der King of Cool und der Prince of Pop. Jazzmusiker Miles Davis (links) mit Popkünstler Andy Warhol am 16. Februar 1987. Genau eine Woche später starb Warhol nach einer Gallenblasenoperation.

Le roi du Kool et le prince du Pop Art. Le musicien de jazz Miles Davis (à gauche) et Andy Warhol, le 16 février 1987. Une semaine plus tard exactement, Warhol mourut des suites d'une opération de la vésicule biliaire.

American artist
Julian Schnabel in
his New York studio,
December 1987.
Behind him is a wall
sculpture of broken
plates.

Der amerikanische
Künstler Julian
Schnabel in seinem
New Yorker Atelier,
Dezember 1987.
Hinter ihm eine
Wandskulptur aus
zerbrochenen Tellern.

L'artiste américain
Julian Schnabel
dans son atelier
new-yorkais,
décembre 1987.
Derrière lui, un mur
sculpté avec des
assiettes cassées.

MARK PETERSON/REUTERS/HULTON|ARCHIVE

BERNARD GOTFRYD/HULTON|ARCHIVE

Golden voices. Luciano Pavarotti (opposite) in a scene from the hugely unsuccessful MGM film *Yes, Giorgio*. (Above) The American soprano Jessye Norman, in a performance of *The Trojans*, 1983.

Goldene Stimmen. (Gegenüberliegende Seite) Luciano Pavarotti in einer Szene des außerordentlich erfolglosen MGM-Films *Yes, Giorgio*. (Oben) Die amerikanische Sopranistin Jessye Norman in einer Aufführung der *Trojaner*, 1983.

Des voix en or. Luciano Pavarotti (ci-contre) dans une scène du film de la MGM *Yes, Giorgio* qui ne rencontra pas le succès escompté. (Ci-dessus) La soprano américaine Jessye Norman dans *Les Troyens*, 1983.

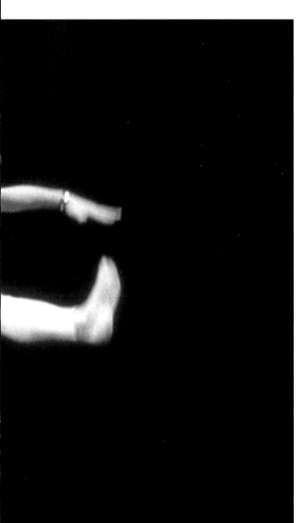

Mikhail Baryshnikov defies gravity as he performs *From Sea to Shining Sea*, New York City, 1981.

Michail Baryshnikov trotzt in *From Sea to Shining Sea* der Schwerkraft, New York City, 1981.

Mikhail Baryshnikov défie les lois de la gravité dans le spectacle intitulé *From Sea to Shining Sea,* New York, 1981.

The American dancer Jeffrey Daniels in costume for Andrew Lloyd Webber's stage musical *Starlight Express*, Apollo Theatre, London, 1980.

Der amerikanische Tänzer Jeffrey Daniels, kostümiert für Andrew Lloyd Webbers Musical *Starlight Express*, Apollo Theatre, London, 1980.

Le danseur américain Jeffrey Daniels en costume dans la comédie musicale *Starlight Express* mise en scène par Andrew Lloyd Webber à l'Appolo Theatre à Londres en 1980.

The Twyla Tharp modern dance company performs the *Golden Section* from the ballet *The Catherine Wheel*, with a score by David Byrne of the new wave band Talking Heads, November 1983.

Die Twyla Tharp Modern Dance Company bei der Aufführung des *Goldenen Schnitts* aus dem Ballett *The Catherine Wheel*. Die Musik stammte von David Byrne von der New-Wave-Band Talking Heads, November 1983.

La compagnie de danse moderne Twyla Tharp interprète *Golden Section,* inclus dans le ballet intitulé *The Catherine Wheel,* sur une musique écrite par David Byrne, membre du groupe new wave Talking Heads, novembre 1983.

The price of fame.
Iranians support the
fatwa and protest
against Rushdie's
book, Beirut
26 February 1989.

Der Preis des
Ruhmes. Iranische
Frauen unterstützen
die Fatwa und
protestieren gegen
Rushdies Buch,
Beirut,
26. Februar 1989.

Le prix de la gloire.
Des Iraniens
soutiennent la fatwa
et manifestent
leur opposition au
livre de Rushdie,
Beyrouth,
26 février 1989.

JAMAL SAIDI/HULTON|ARCHIVE

The product of genius. Salman Rushdie with a copy of *The Satanic Verses*, the book that could have cost him his life, 17 February 1989.

Das Werk des Meisters. Salman Rushdie mit einem Exemplar seines Romans *Die satanischen Verse,* des Buches, das ihn das Leben hätte kosten können, 17. Februar 1989.

L'œuvre du génie. Salman Rushdie avec une copie des *Versets sataniques*, le livre qui aurait pu lui coûter la vie, le 17 février 1989.

American playwright, film writer and director David Mamet, 1985. Mamet's huge contribution to both stage and screen in the 1980s included *Glengarry Glen Ross* and *Speed the Plow*.

Der amerikanische Dramatiker, Filmautor und Regisseur David Mamet, 1985. Zu seinen wichtigsten Leistungen der achtziger Jahre für Bühne und Leinwand gehörten *Glengarry Glen Ross* und *Speed the Plow*.

L'Américain David Mamet, dramaturge, scénariste et réalisateur, 1985. Il contribua de manière prolifique au théâtre et au cinéma durant les années 1980 avec, notamment, *Glengarry Glen Ross* et *Speed the Plow*.

Sam Shepard,
American dramatist
and actor, with
friend, November
1980. Shepard's
major works in the
1980s included
Lie of the Mind and
the screenplay for
the much acclaimed
1984 film
Paris, Texas.

Sam Shepard,
der amerikanische
Dramatiker und
Schauspieler, im
November 1980 mit
einem vierbeinigen
Kameraden. Zu
Shepards wichtig-
sten Leistungen der
achtziger Jahre
gehörten *Lie of the
Mind* und das Dreh-
buch für den stark
beachteten Film
Paris, Texas (1984).

L'Américain Sam
Shepard, drama-
turge et acteur,
avec son chien,
novembre 1980.
Les principales
œuvres de Shepard
durant les années
1980 comprennent
Lie of the Mind et le
scénario du film
Paris, Texas, qui
connut un très grand
succès public et
critique en 1984.

Defying convention…
The English writer
and commentator
Quentin Crisp,
with his 37-year-
old gas stove,
Chelsea, London,
14 August 1981.

Keine Rücksicht auf
Konventionen …
Der englische Schrift-
steller und Kommen-
tator Quentin Crisp
neben seinem 37
Jahre alten Gasherd,
Chelsea, London,
14. August 1981.

Défiant les conven-
tions … L'écrivain et
critique anglais
Quentin Crisp
devant sa cuisinière
à gaz, achetée
37 ans plus tôt,
Chelsea, Londres,
14 août 1981.

Tama Janowitz, author of *Slaves of New York*, takes time out from a Halloween party at the Salon des Artistes, SoHo, New York City, October 1987.

Tama Janowitz, Autorin von *Großstadtsklaven*, bei einer Erholungspause während einer Halloween-Party im Salon des Artistes, SoHo, New York City, Oktober 1987.

Tama Janowitz, auteur de *Slaves of New York*, prend un bol d'air frais en pleine fête de Halloween au Salon des Artistes, dans le quartier de SoHo à New York, octobre 1987.

JEFFREY AARONSON/COLORIFIC!

Bold, brash, anti-establishment and highly idiosyncratic: American writer Hunter S Thompson, Aspen, Colorado. Thompson invented the style of subjective journalism he labelled 'Gonzo'.

Unerschrocken, unverfroren, sehr eigenwillig, ein Feind des Establishments: der amerikanische Autor Hunter S. Thompson in Aspen, Colorado. Thompson erfand jenen subjektiven journalistischen Stil, den er als „Gonzo" bezeichnete.

Audacieux, effronté, anti-establishement et mono-maniaque : l'écrivain américain, Hunter S. Thomson, à Aspen, Colorado. Thompson inventa un style de journalisme subjectif qu'il appela « Gonzo ».

William Burroughs, one-time spokesman for the 'Beat Generation', arrives in Madison, Wisconsin, for a reading from his works, 1982.

William Burroughs, einst der Sprecher der Beat-Generation, bei der Ankunft zu einer Lesung aus seinen Büchern, Madison, Wisconsin, 1982.

Arrivée de William Burroughs, ancien chef de file de la Beat generation, à Madison, Wisconsin, pour une lecture de son œuvre, 1982.

JOE McNALLY/WHEELER/COLORIFIC!

ANTHONY SUAU/BLACK STAR/COLORIFIC!

Writer P J O'Rourke on the front line in South Korea, 1987. In the 1980s, O'Rourke wrote for many magazines (including *Rolling Stone, Playboy* and *Esquire*) and also published *Modern Manners* and *Republican Party Reptile*.

Autor P. J. O'Rourke an der Frontlinie, Südkorea, 1987. In den achtziger Jahren schrieb O'Rourke für viele Zeitschriften (unter anderem *Rolling Stone, Playboy* und *Esquire*) und veröffentlichte die Bücher *Modern Manners* und *Republican Party Reptile*.

L'écrivain P. J. O'Rourke en première ligne en Corée du Sud, 1987. Dans les années 1980, O'Rourke écrivit pour de nombreux magazines (dont *Rolling Stone, Playboy* et *Esquire*) et publia également *Modern Manners* et *Republican Party Reptile*.

The English novelist Martin Amis in the Portobello Road, Notting Hill, London, 1989. Amis drew much of his inspiration from the streets of London.

Der englische Romancier Martin Amis in der Portobello Road im Londoner Stadtteil Notting Hill, 1989. Amis ließ sich stark von den Straßen Londons inspirieren.

Le romancier anglais Martin Amis à Portobello Road, Notting Hill, Londres, 1989. Amis trouvait son inspiration principalement dans les rues de Londres.

So little to do, so much time to do it… Tom Wolfe was less than prolific in the 1980s. He published only one novel – *The Bonfire of the Vanities* (1988) – but it was a huge success.

So wenig zu tun, so viel Zeit … Tom Wolfe war in den achtziger Jahren alles andere als fruchtbar. Er veröffentlichte nur einen Roman – *Fegefeuer der Eitelkeiten* (1988) – aber der wurde ein großer Erfolg.

Si peu à dire, si long à écrire … Tom Wolfe ne fut guère prolifique au cours de la décennie. Il publia un seul roman, *Le bûcher des vanités* (1988), mais ce fut un énorme succès.

HENRY GROSSMAN/COLORIFIC!

Death in the kitchen… American horror writer Stephen King brandishes a lobster, 1983. The knives on the wall may be for more than culinary purposes. King was perhaps the most commercially successful writer in the 1980s.

Der Tod lauert in der Küche … Amerikas Horrorspezialist Stephen King schwingt den Hummer, 1983. Ob die Messer an der Wand wirklich nur Küchenzwecken dienen? King war kommerziell der vielleicht erfolgreichste Schriftsteller der achtziger Jahre.

Mort en cuisine … L'Américain Stephen King, auteur de livres d'épouvante, brandit un homard, 1983. Est-il possible que les couteaux accrochés au mur servent à autre chose que faire la cuisine ? King est probablement l'écrivain qui connut le plus grand succès commercial des années 1980.

7. Pop
Pop
Pop

'It's like a jungle sometimes…' Pioneering rapper Grandmaster Flash and his Bronx-based group the Furious Five were the premier DJ-rap team of the early 1980s. These words, taken from his rap *The Message*, introduced rap's preoccupations: urban fear and loathing.

„Manchmal ist es wie im Dschungel …" Rap-Pionier Grandmaster Flash und seine aus der Bronx stammende Gruppe, die Furious Five, waren die erste DJ-Rap-Band der frühen achtziger Jahre. Diese Zeile aus seinem Rapsong *The Message* benennt typische Themen dieser Musikrichtung: Furcht und Abscheu in der Großstadt.

«Y'a des jours c'est comme la jungle … » Le pionnier du rap, Grandmaster Flash et son groupe du Bronx, les Furious Five, furent le premier groupe DJ-rap du début des années 1980. Ces paroles, extraites de sa chanson *The Message,* reflètent les préoccupations des rappeurs : peur et haine urbaines.

7. Pop
Pop
Pop

The days of vinyl were numbered. Stocks of cassettes dwindled on the shelves of record stores but the introduction of the CD and the pop video was a shot in the arm for the music industry. Sales and profits spiralled; the incidence of fame and celebrity status reached all-time highs.

In Britain late in 1984, Band Aid released the single *Do They Know It's Christmas?* The £8 million proceeds from the sales of the single went to relieve starving millions in Ethiopia. In summer 1985 came the Global Jukebox, the simultaneous Live Aid concerts in Wembley Stadium, London and the JFK Stadium, Philadelphia. The concerts raised $70 million dollars, not enough alas to solve the worsening problems in even one corner of Africa. But it brought the world together, blazed a path through the jungle of pop, and awakened the consciences of pop stars for the rest of the century.

Apart from Band Aid/Live Aid, there were other things happening in music: electronic, New Romantic, Stock, Aitken and Waterman, Garage, hip hop/rap, Acid House – all had their place in the sun…

Die Tage der Vinylscheibe waren gezählt. Die Kassettenstapel in den Plattengeschäften schmolzen; die Einführung der Compact Disc und der Videoclips gaben der Musikindustrie mächtigen Auftrieb. Die Verkaufszahlen und Profite schossen in die Höhe; Starruhm und Starkult erreichten einen nie erklommenen Gipfel.

In Großbritannien brachte Ende 1984 Band Aid die Single *Do They Know It's Christmas?* heraus. Die acht Millionen Pfund aus dem Verkauf der Single gingen in die Hilfe für die Millionen Hungernden in Äthiopien. Im Sommer 1985 folgte die Global Jukebox, die zeitgleichen Live-Aid-Konzerte im Londoner Wembleystadion und im

JFK Stadium von Philadelphia. Die Konzerte spielten stolze 70 Millionen Dollar ein; mehr als einen Tropfen auf den heißen Stein bedeutete dies angesichts der immer schlimmer werdenden Lage in vielen Teilen Afrikas jedoch nicht. Aber sie brachten die Welt zusammen, schlugen einen Pfad durch den Popdschungel und weckten das Bewusstsein der Popstars für die Probleme der Welt.

Neben Band Aid/Live Aid gab es natürlich noch vieles andere in der Popmusik: Electronic, New Romantic, Stock, Aitken and Waterman, Garage, Hip-Hop/Rap, Acid House – alles fand seinen Platz …

Les jours du vinyle étaient comptés. Les stocks de cassettes diminuaient dans les rayons des disquaires, mais l'arrivée du CD et de la vidéo pop permit de réanimer une industrie de la musique défaillante. Les ventes et les bénéfices augmentèrent de manière vertigineuse, engendrant un nombre record de gloires et de célébrités.

À la fin 1984, en Grande-Bretagne, Band Aid sortit un 45 tours intitulé *Do They Know It's Christmas?* Les bénéfices tirés des ventes du disque s'élevèrent à 8 millions de livres sterling et furent versés à une association pour les victimes de la famine en Éthiopie. En été 1985, il y eut le fameux Global Jukebox, avec des concerts Live Aid organisés simultanément au stade de Wembley à Londres et au stade J. F. Kennedy à Philadelphie. Les concerts permirent de récolter 70 millions de dollars, pas assez malheureusement pour soulager l'Afrique de ses problèmes toujours plus graves. Toutefois, ce mouvement de solidarité réussit à rassembler le monde, frayant un chemin à travers la jungle de la musique rock et éveillant les consciences des rock stars pour le restant du siècle.

À part Band Aid/Live Aid, les courants musicaux ne manquaient pas : électronique, nouveau romantique, Stock, Aitken et Waterman, Garage, hip hop/rap, Acid House – tous réussissaient à se faire une place au soleil …

(Left) The crowd at Wembley Stadium, London, for the Live Aid concert, 13 July 1985. (Above, left to right) George Michael, Bob Geldof and David Bowie.

(Links) Die Menge im Londoner Wembleystadion während des Live-Aid-Konzerts am 13. Juli 1985. (Oben, von links nach rechts) George Michael, Bob Geldof und David Bowie.

(À gauche) La foule du stade de Wembley à Londres pour le concert Live Aid, le 13 juillet 1985. (Ci-dessus, de gauche à droite) George Michael, Bob Geldof et David Bowie.

More Live Aid stars.
Freddie Mercury
with Queen at
Wembley. The event
raised $70 million
for famine victims
in Africa.

Noch ein Star für
Live Aid. Freddie
Mercury mit seiner
Band Queen im
Wembleystadion.
Das Event spielte
70 Millionen Dollar
für die Opfer
des Hungers in
Afrika ein.

D'autres stars du
concert Live Aid.
Freddie Mercury
et les Queen à
Wembley. Le concert
permit de récolter
70 millions de
dollars pour les
victimes de la famine
en Éthiopie.

Madonna getting
into the groove at
the Live Aid concert
in Philadelphia,
Pennsylvania, also
on 13 July 1985.

Madonna groovt
sich ein. Szene vom
Live-Aid-Konzert
in Philadelphia,
Pennsylvania, das
zeitgleich mit dem
Londoner Konzert
am 13. Juli 1985
stattfand.

Madonna dans le
sillon du concert
Live Aid à Philadel-
phie, aux États-Unis,
également le
13 juillet 1985.

Prince in his purple period storms through a number from his hit film and album of 1984, *Purple Rain*.

Seine Purpurzeit. Prince bei einer Nummer aus seinem Film und gleichnamigen Album *Purple Rain*, einem Hit des Jahres 1984.

Prince en pleine période pourpre joua un morceau de *Purple Rain*, extrait de son film et album qui furent un énorme succès, 1984.

Michael Jackson on tour in London following the release of 1987's *Bad*. The album generated five separate Number 1 hits for him.

Michael Jackson in London auf der Tournee nach der Veröffentlichung von *Bad* (1987). Fünf Songs des Albums erreichten die Nummer 1 in den Charts.

Michael Jackson en tournée à Londres après la sortie de *Bad*, son album de 1987. Ce disque lui valut d'être cinq fois n° 1 au hit-parade.

The Stones roll on and on... Mick Jagger (left) with Ron Wood, in concert 1981. 'Everything going on,' he said, 'I've seen at least twice before.'

Und die Steine rollen weiter ... Mick Jagger (links) mit Ron Wood bei einem Konzert, 1981. „Alles, was neu ist", sagt Jagger, „habe ich wenigstens schon zweimal erlebt."

Les Stones continuent de rouler leur bosse ... Mick Jagger (à gauche) avec Ron Wood en concert, 1981. «Tout ce qui se passe aujourd'hui, je l'ai déjà vu au moins deux fois », déclara-t-il.

David Bowie
on tour with
Tin Machine, 1989.
He formed the band
that year with
ex-Stooges Tony
and Hunt Sales,
and the guitarist
Reeves Gabrels.

David Bowie mit Tin
Machine auf Tour,
1989. Diese Band
wurde im gleichen
Jahr gegründet. Mit
dabei Ex-Stooges
Tony und Hunt Sales
sowie Gitarrist
Reeves Gabrels.

David Bowie en
tournée avec Tin
Machine, groupe
qu'il forma en 1989
avec Tony et Hunt
Sales, anciens de
Stooges, et le guita-
riste Reeves Gabrels.

LESTER COHEN/SHOOTING STAR/COLORIFIC!

One of the biggest stars of the 1980s MTV era, Cyndi Lauper. Her huge hit *Girls Just Wanna Have Fun* later became the basis of several advertising campaigns.

Einer der MTV-Superstars der achtziger Jahre: Cyndi Lauper. Auf ihrem Hit *Girls Just Wanna Have Fun* wurden ganze Reklamekampagnen aufgebaut.

Cyndi Lauper, une des plus grandes stars de l'époque MTV des années 1980. Sa chanson *Girls Just Wanna Have Fun* fut un succès énorme avant d'être reprise dans de nombreuses campagnes publicitaires.

Whitney Houston, whose eponymous first album hit the charts at Number 1 and sold more than 14 million copies.

Whitney Houston. Ihr gleichnamiges erstes Albums wurde zur Nummer 1 in den Charts und ging mehr als 14 Millionen Mal über den Ladentisch.

Whitney Houston dont le disque éponyme devint n° 1 au hit-parade et fut vendu à 14 millions d'exemplaires.

DIANA LYN/SHOOTING STAR/COLORIFIC!

Robert Palmer, the Dapper Dan of Eighties rock. His biggest success was *Addicted to Love*, from his 1985 solo album *Riptide*.

Robert Palmer, der Geschniegelte unter den Rockstars der achtziger Jahre. Sein größter Erfolg war *Addicted to Love* aus seinem Soloalbum *Riptide* (1985).

Robert Palmer, le Dapper Dan du rock des années 1980. Son plus gros succès fut *Addicted to Love*, de son album solo de 1985 intitulé *Riptide*.

Dave Stewart (left) and Annie Lennox of the Eurythmics spread the message in their Katherine Hamnett T-shirts at Fashion Aid.

Dave Stewart (links) und Annie Lennox von den Eurythmics verbreiten mit ihren Katherine-Hamnett-T-Shirts auf der Veranstaltung Fashion Aid ihre Botschaft.

Dave Stewart (à gauche) et Annie Lennox du groupe Eurythmics font passer le message sur leurs T-shirts conçus par Katherine Hamnett pour un spectacle de charité, Fashion Aid.

COLORIFIC!

Marvin Lee Aday, aka Meat Loaf, gives his considerable all on stage in the 1980s. They were not good years for the superstar. After *Bad Attitude* and *Blind Before I Stop* bombed, he filed for bankruptcy.

Marvin Lee Aday, besser bekannt als Meat Loaf, entfaltete in den achtziger Jahren auf der Bühne wuchtige Präsenz. Es waren aber keine guten Jahre für den Superstar. Nach dem Reinfall mit *Bad Attitude* und *Blind Before I Stop* musste er Konkurs anmelden.

L'impressionnant Marvin Lee Aday, alias Meat Loaf, sur scène. Les années 1980 ne furent pas très bonnes pour la superstar. Après l'échec de *Bad Attitude* et de *Blind Before I Stop*, il dut déclarer faillite.

The Boss comes home. Bruce Springsteen on stage in his home state, New Jersey, August 1985, the year of *Born in the USA*.

Der Boss kommt nach Hause. Bruce Springsteen auf der Bühne in seinem Heimatstaat New Jersey, August 1985. Im selben Jahr erschien *Born in the USA*.

Le Boss rentre au bercail. Bruce Springsteen sur scène dans son état natal, le New Jersey, août 1985, l'année de *Born in the USA*.

FRATKIN/SIPA PRESS

The joys of touring… Luke and Matt Goss greet the dawn in the comfort of their limousine, 1989.

Die Freuden einer Tournee … Luke und Matt Goss begrüßen in ihrer Luxuslimousine den Sonnenaufgang, 1989.

Les joies des tournées … Luke et Matt Goss saluent le lever du jour en baillant, confortablement installés dans une limousine, 1989.

TONY MOTT/S.I.N.

They evolved in the world-weary late 1970s with a cover version of *Satisfaction* they sang wearing industrial cleaning outfits, but Devo (above) believed that the world was de-evolving into increasingly dysfunctional societies.

Sie kamen in den weltverdrossenen späten siebziger Jahren mit einer Coverversion von *Satisfaction* nach oben, die sie in Schutzanzügen für Reinigungspersonal sangen, trotzdem glaubte Devo (oben), dass die Welt in immer weniger funktionierende Gesellschaften zerfallen würde.

Ils traversèrent le monde fatigué de la fin des années 1970 avec une adaptation de *Satisfaction* et chantèrent en bleus de travail. Selon Devo (ci-dessus), le monde produisait des sociétés dont les dysfonctionnements ne cessaient de croître.

KATIA NATOZA/S.I.N.

Less cynical and more melodic were Bon Jovi (above), led by Jon Bon Jovi (centre). Combining mainstream hard rock with metal, the band had great success with *Slippery When Wet* (1986) and *New Jersey* (1988).

Harmloser und melodischer war die Gruppe Bon Jovi (oben) mit ihrem Leader Jon Bon Jovi (Mitte). In der Verbindung von Mainstream Hard Rock und Heavy Metal hatte die Band große Erfolge mit *Slippery When Wet* (1986) und *New Jersey* (1988).

Moins cyniques et plus mélodieux, les Bon Jovi (ci-dessus) menés par Jon Bon Jovi (au centre). Associant le hard rock grand public au heavy metal, le groupe connut un grand succès avec *Slippery When Wet* (1986) et *New Jersey* (1988).

TERENCE SPENCER/COLORIFIC!

(Above) The Police on set for their video single *Synchronicity* (1983) – (left to right) Andy Summers, Sting and Stewart Copeland. (Opposite) Duran Duran pose for a still while filming their video *Wild Boy*s (1984).

(Oben) The Police in den Kulissen ihres Videoclips zu *Synchronicity* (1983) – Andy Summers, Sting und Stewart Copeland (von links nach rechts). (Gegenüberliegende Seite) Duran Duran posieren für ein Foto bei der Verfilmung ihres Videos *Wild Boys* (1984).

(Ci-dessus) Police sur le tournage de la vidéo de *Synchronicity* (1983) – (de gauche à droite) Andy Summers, Sting et Stewart Copeland. (Ci-contre) Portrait du groupe Duran Duran sur le tournage du clip de *Wild Boys* (1984).

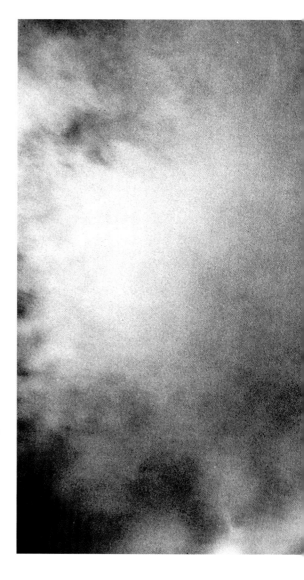

Straight outta Compton. South Central LA
rapper Ice-T starts the body count on stage in
London, 1989.

Direkt aus Compton. Der Rapper Ice-T
aus South Central Los Angeles zählt aus.
Bühnenauftritt in London, 1989.

Tout droit sorti de Compton, South Central
à Los Angeles, le rappeur Ice-T entame un
compte à rebours sur une scène londonienne,
1989.

Chuck D (fist clenched) and Flavor Flav (front, centre) of Public Enemy 'bum rush' the show at the Apollo, Manchester, 1989.

Chuck D (mit geballter Faust) und Flavor Flav (in der Mitte vorn) von Public Enemy heizen im Apollo ein, Manchester, 1989.

Chuck D (poing serré) et Flavor Flav (devant, au centre) mettent de l'ambiance à l'Apollo, Manchester, 1989.

(Left to right) Flavor Flav, LL Cool J and DJ Bobcat. LL's knack for making hip hop accessible led to accusations of selling out. Later he successfully turned his career to film and television.

Flavor Flav, LL Cool J und DJ Bobcat (von links nach rechts). LLs Talent, den Hip-Hop zugänglicher zu machen, trug ihm den Vorwurf des Ausverkaufs ein. Später wandte er sich erfolgreich Film und Fernsehen zu.

(De gauche à droite) Flavor Flav, LL Cool J et DJ Bobcat. Pour avoir rendu le hip hop accessible à tous, LL fut accusé de tromper les siens. Par la suite, il se reconvertit avec succès dans le cinéma et la télévision.

Getting his shirt lifted, Morrissey sings on with The Smiths at a gig at the Liverpool Corn Exhange, February 1986.

Auch wenn man ihm das Hemd vom Leib reißt, Morrissey singt weiter. Auftritt von The Smiths in der Liverpool Corn Exchange, Februar 1986.

Se faire tirer par la chemise. Morrissey chante avec les Smith lors d'un concert au Liverpool Corn Exchange, février 1986.

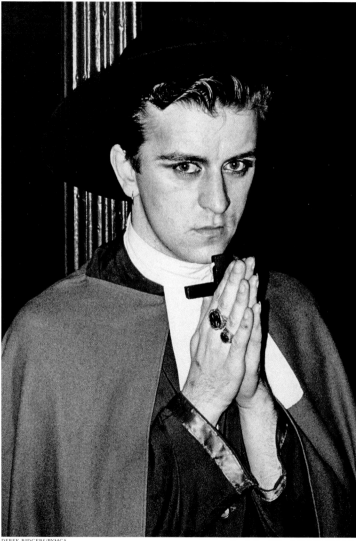

Friends and admirers. (Left) Steve Strange prays outside the gates of the Hell club, 1980. Ahead lay success, rather than damnation, with *Fade to Grey*.

Friends and Admirers. (Links) Steve Strange betet vor den Pforten des Hell Club, 1980. Vor ihm lag nicht die Verdammnis, sondern der Erfolg mit *Fade to Grey*.

Amis et admirateurs. (À gauche) Steve Strange prie devant les portes du club nommé Hell (enfer), 1980. Le succès, plutôt que la damnation, allait suivre avec *Fade to Grey*.

Boy George outside
the entrance to
Le Beat Route club,
Soho, London,
1981. Ahead lay
success with Culture
Club's *Do You
Really Want to
Hurt Me?*

Boy George vor dem
Eingang des Le Beat
Route Club, Soho,
London, 1981.
Vor ihm und seiner
Band Culture Club
lag der Erfolg von
*Do You Really Want
to Hurt Me?*

Boy George devant
l'entrée du Beat
Route club, dans le
quartier de Soho à
Londres, 1981.
Le succès n'allait
pas tarder non plus
avec la chanson du
groupe Culture
Club, *Do You Really
Want to Hurt Me ?*

DEREK RIDGERS/PYMCA

Australian singer,
songwriter and
novelist Nick Cave,
founder and leader
of the Bad Seeds,
in introspective
mood, 1985.

In nachdenklicher
Stimmung: der
australische Sänger,
Songschreiber und
Romancier Nick
Cave, Gründer und
Leader der Bad
Seeds, 1985.

L'Australien Nick
Cave – le chanteur,
parolier et roman-
cier qui fonda et
dirigea le groupe
Bad Seeds – plongé
dans ses pensées,
1985.

Adam Ant applies
war paint before
going on stage,
1981. It was the
year of *Stand and
Deliver* and *Prince
Charming*.

Adam Ant legt vor
dem Gang auf die
Bühne die Kriegs-
bemalung an, 1981.
Im gleichen Jahr
kamen *Stand and
Deliver* und *Prince
Charming* heraus.

Séance de
maquillage et
peinture de guerre
pour Adam Ant
avant de monter
sur scène, 1981.
Ce fut l'année de
Stand and Deliver et
de *Prince Charming*.

Robert Smith, leader of The Cure, in typically ghoulish mode, though without his trademark lipstick smudge.

Robert Smith, der Sänger von The Cure, vampiresk wie immer, aber ohne sein Markenzeichen, den verschmierten Lippenstift.

Robert Smith, le chanteur de The Cure, d'humeur macabre comme d'habitude mais sans sa marque patentée, le fameux rouge à lèvres noir.

IAN TILTON/S.I.N.

Siouxsie Sioux of
Siouxsie and the
Banshees, one of the
longest lasting of the
1970s-spawned
punk bands.

Siouxsie Sioux von
Siouxsie and the
Banshees, einer der
langlebigsten der
vielen Punkbands
der siebziger Jahre.

Siouxsie Sioux de
Siouxsie and the
Banshees, un des
groupes punks des
années 1970 qui
sut durer plus long-
temps que les autres.

PETER ANDERSON/S.I.N.

8. Fashion
Die Mode
La mode

Princess Diana steps out at the British première of Robert Zemeckis's *Back to the Future*, 1985. By this time she had abandoned her Sloane Ranger look for a far more sophisticated wardrobe.

Prinzessin Diana beim Verlassen der britischen Premiere von Robert Zemeckis' *Zurück in die Zukunft,* 1985. Zu dieser Zeit hatte sie ihr Sekretärin-auf-Ausgang-Outfit aufgegeben und zog Raffinierteres vor.

La princesse Diana quittant la première britannique du film de Robert Zemeckis, *Back to the Future,* 1985. Elle avait enfin abandonné le look « Sloane Ranger », style BCBG propre à un quartier chic de Londres, pour une garde-robe plus raffinée.

8. Fashion
Die Mode
La mode

Whereas the Seventies had their fashion trademarks in the mini and the punk, no particular style typified the 1980s. Instead, they had an icon – Diana, Princess of Wales. Shy and jejune when she first appeared towards the end of the 1970s, by the time she married Prince Charles in July 1981 Diana (and her wedding dress) had captured the imagination of women everywhere. By the end of the decade, her style and influence had spread all over the world.

In the fashion houses there were few changes. The established names – Courrèges, Saint Laurent, Gucci, Armani, Westwood, Lagerfeld and a dozen more – still held sway over the catwalks of Paris, Milan, New York and London. But there were also relative newcomers, among them Katharine Hamnett, Christian Lacroix, Caroline Charles and, at the forefront of Japanese designers, Issey Miyake and Comme des Garçons.

Meanwhile, out on the streets, fashions continued to mutate and became harder to pin down. The Doc Marten boot, that old stand-by of the Seventies, was given high-fashion status on the catwalk before it returned to the street as a shoe.

Während die siebziger Jahre mit Mini und Punk ihre klar erkennbaren Modestile besaßen, gab es keinen spezifischen Stil der achtziger Jahre. Dafür aber gab es ein Leitbild – Diana, die Prinzessin von Wales. Als sie Ende der siebziger Jahre auf der Bühne der Öffentlichkeit erschien, war sie schüchtern und unscheinbar, doch als sie im Juli 1981 Prinz Charles heiratete, beschäftigte Diana (und ihr Hochzeitskleid) bereits weltweit die Phantasien der Frauen. Am Ende des Jahrzehnts hatte ihr Stil auf der ganzen Welt Schule gemacht.

In den Modehäusern gab es nur wenige Veränderungen. Die Laufstege in Paris, Mailand, New York und London wurden weiterhin von den etablierten Namen beherrscht: Courrèges, Saint Laurent, Gucci, Armani, Westwood, Lagerfeld und einem Dutzend weiterer Couturiers. Es gab aber auch einige, die als Newcomer gelten konnten, darunter Katharine Hamnett, Christian Lacroix, Caroline Charles und, als Avantgarde der japanischen Modeschöpfer, Issey Miyake und Comme des Garçons.

Auf der Straße veränderte sich die Mode und wurde schwerer bestimmbar. Der Springerstiefel, das Fossil der siebziger Jahre, erklomm den Laufsteg der eleganten Mode und kehrte dann als Schuh auf die Straße zurück.

Alors que les années soixante-dix furent caractérisées par la minijupe et la mode punk, aucun style vestimentaire ne s'imposa dans les années quatre-vingt. Par contre, cette décennie créa une icône avec Diana, princesse de Galles. Timide et ennuyeuse lors de ses premières apparitions à la fin des années soixante-dix, Diana en robe de mariée séduit l'imaginaire des femmes du monde entier au moment de son mariage avec le prince Charles en juillet 1981. À la fin de la décennie, son style était copié dans le monde entier.

Dans les maisons de couture, peu de changements intervinrent. Les grands noms, Courrèges, Saint Laurent, Gucci, Armani, Westwood, Lagerfeld et une douzaine d'autres, continuaient de tenir le haut du pavé dans les défilés à Paris, Milan, New York et Londres. Mais des nouveaux venus, plus ou moins connus, réussirent à percer. Parmi eux, il y avait Katharine Hamnett, Christian Lacroix, Caroline Charles et, au premier plan des couturiers japonais, Issey Miyake et Comme des Garçons.

Pendant ce temps, dans la rue, la mode continuait à évoluer et devenait toujours plus difficile à cataloguer. La Doc Marten, chaussure banale des années soixante-dix, devint un objet de haute couture sur les passerelles des défilés avant de redescendre dans la rue et de réintégrer son statut de simple botte.

A glum Diana visits
a Huddersfield
youth centre,
22 March 1982.
That cup of tea
proves to be a useless
fashion accessory.

Verdrossen.
Prinzessin Diana
beim Besuch eines
Jugendzentrums
in Huddersfield,
22. März 1982. Die
Teetasse als abwegi-
ges Modeaccessoire.

Une Diana morne
en visite dans un
centre pour jeunes à
Huddersfield, le
22 mars 1982. Cette
tasse de thé est un
accessoire de mode
tout à fait superflu.

Power dressing, royal style… Diana at a wedding in 1983. Neither her mother-in-law nor her sister-in-law could match such swagger.

Großer Auftritt im königlichen Stile … Prinzessin Diana bei einer Hochzeit, 1983. Weder ihre Schwiegermutter noch ihre Schwägerin konnten da modisch mithalten.

Tenue séduisante et style royal … Diana lors d'un mariage en 1983. Ni sa belle-mère, ni sa belle-sœur ne surent jamais dégager un tel chic.

Giorgio Armani, 1987. Although Armani was big on wide, padded shoulders, they were never as big as the coat-hanger suggests.

Giorgio Armani, 1987. Obwohl Armani breite, ausgepolsterte Schultern liebte – so massiv, wie der Kleiderbügel glauben macht, waren seine Kreationen auch wieder nicht.

Giorgio Armani, 1987. Certes, Armani aimait les costumes aux épaules larges et rembourrées, mais il n'en conçut jamais d'aussi larges que ce cintre.

Gianni Versace and dummy at home on Lake Como, June 1983. Those looking for subtlety and minimalism would not find them in Versace's designs.

Gianni Versace mit Kleiderpuppe in seinem Zuhause am Comer See, Juni 1983. Wer Subtilität und Schlichtheit suchte, war bei Versace nicht an der richtigen Adresse.

Gianni Versace avec un mannequin dans sa maison au bord du lac de Côme, juin 1983. Les adeptes de style à la fois discret et raffiné n'auraient pas trouvé leur bonheur chez Versace.

Issey Miyake proves the truth of Coco Chanel's claim that 'fashion is architecture' with this heavy item of knitwear, 1982.

Issey Miyake stellt mit wulstigen Strickkreationen die Wahrheit von Coco Chanels Aussage „Mode ist Architektur" unter Beweis, 1982.

Avec cet impression-nant pull en laine, Issey Miyake démontre que Coco Chanel avait raison quand elle disait que « la mode est architecture », 1982.

Some designs creat-
ed by Miyake (right)
were mounted on
sculptural wire that
allowed them to
stand out from the
body.

Manche der Schöp-
fungen Miyakes
(rechts) waren auf
Drahtgestelle mon-
tiert, um vom Kör-
per abzustehen.

Certaines des pièces
créées par Miyake
(à droite) étaient
montées sur des
structures sculptées
au fil de fer pour ne
pas plaquer au corps.

Model turned
actress Lauren
Hutton adopts a rich
disco look for the
1980 Academy
Awards ceremony,
Los Angeles.

Schauspielerin und
Ex-Model Lauren
Hutton entschied
sich bei der Oscar-
Verleihung 1980
in Los Angeles für
den glitzernden
Disco-Look.

Lauren Hutton,
mannequin devenue
actrice, adopte un
style disco peu
discret pour la céré-
monie des oscars de
1980 à Los Angeles.

Michelle Pfeiffer as she appeared in the 1983 Brian de Palma movie *Scarface*. For some reason, Pfeiffer thought she had a face like a duck.

Michelle Pfeiffer in Brian de Palmas Film *Scarface*, 1983. Aus irgendeinem Grund glaubte sie, ihr Gesicht hätte Ähnlichkeit mit einer Ente.

Michelle Pfeiffer, telle qu'elle apparut dans *Scarface*, le film de Brian de Palma réalisé en 1983. Pour une raison ou pour une autre, Pfeiffer trouvait qu'elle avait une tête de canard.

Couture meets casual. Cybil Shepherd, star of TV's *Moonlighting*, wears trainers with an evening dress. Nice.

Haute Couture und Alltag. Fernsehstar Cybil Shepherd *(Das Model und der Schnüffler)* trägt Trainingsschuhe zum Abendkleid. Niedlich.

Chic et décontracté. Cybil Shepherd, vedette de la série de télévision *Moonlighting,* porte des baskets avec sa robe de soirée. C'est très joli !

A stone-washed,
pre-ripped,
Footloose Sarah
Jessica Parker just
wanted to have fun.

Die Hose stone-
washed und
aufgerissen: Sarah
Jessica Parker
(Footloose) wollte
nur Spaß haben.

Style délavé et
déchiré pour Sarah
Jessica Parker de
Footloose qui ne
cherchait qu'à
s'amuser.

DIANA LYN/SHOOTING STAR/COLORIFIC!

The leisurewear fashion. Jamie Lee Curtis in work-out mode for the 1985 James Bridges film *Perfect*.

Freizeitmode. Jamie Lee Curtis betätigt sich sportlich in dem James-Bridges-Film *Perfect* von 1985.

La mode des vêtements de sport. Jamie Lee Curtis en tenue d'entraînement pour *Perfect*, le film de James Bridges, 1985.

Linda Evans, soapy
star of the 1980s
TV hit *Dynasty*,
in obligatory
headband, leotard
and leggings at her
private gym, 1983.

Linda Evans, Star
der in den achtziger
Jahren erfolgreichen
Seifenoper *Denver
Clan*, mit obligato-
rischem Stirnband,
Trikot und
Gamaschen in
ihrem privaten
Sportstudio, 1983.

Linda Evans, vedette
mielleuse de la série
TV *Dynasty,* grand
succès des années
1980, pose dans
sa salle de gym
privée dans la tenue
qui s'impose :
collants, jambières
et bandeau, 1983.

ABC TV/HULTON|ARCHIVE

Madonna in concert, 1985. Her studied 'couldn't care less' look was widely copied.

Madonna bei einem Konzertauftritt, 1985. Ihr gekonnt gleichgültiges Erscheinungsbild wurde weltweit nachgeahmt.

Madonna en concert, 1985. Son style « m'en-foutiste » fut beaucoup copié.

LAURA LEVINE/VISAGES/COLORIFIC!

Madonna gave wannabes a look to follow for a year or so, one characterised by trousers or mini skirt, lacy tops, necklaces and oversized knitwear. The look offered liberation without stigma.

Madonna lieferte den Trendbewussten ein Modevorbild, dem sie ein oder zwei Jahre folgten. Charakteristisch waren Hosen oder Miniröcke, Oberteile mit Spitzen, Halsketten und übergroße Stricksachen. Dieser Look versprach Befreiung ohne Stigma.

Madonna offrit à ses fans un style qui dura un an environ et qui consistait à porter des pantalons ou une minijupe avec un haut en dentelles, un tricot trop grand et un collier. Avec ce style, la tenue était sexy sans être choquante.

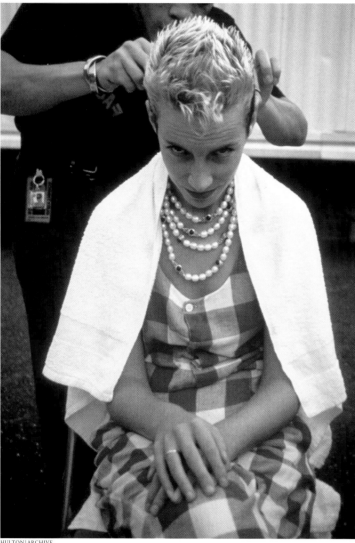

Annie Lennox gets her Eurythmics crop renewed for the Sweet Dreams Tour of 1983–4.

Annie Lennox lässt sich ihren Eurythmics-Stoppel-schnitt für die Sweet-Dreams-Tournee von 1983/84 erneuern.

Séance de coiffure pour Annie Lennox dont la coupe de cheveux courts caractérisait le style Eurythmics durant la tournée intitulée Sweet Dreams en 1983–84.

Blonde with ambition. By 1986 Madonna had changed her image yet again: this was the way she looked on the cover of *True Blue*.

Blondine mit Ehrgeiz. 1986 änderte Madonna mal wieder ihr Image. So erschien sie auf dem Cover von *True Blue*.

Blonde d'ambition. En 1986, Madonna changea à nouveau son image. C'est ce look qu'elle choisit pour faire la couverture de son album *True Blue*.

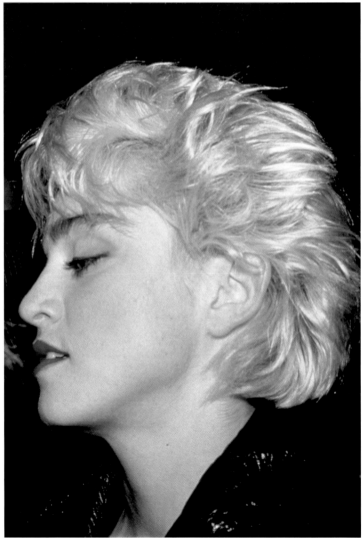

JOHN REARDON/THE OBSERVER/HULTON|ARCHIVE

Punk was reborn in the mid-Eighties as a big bold (commercial) fashion statement. In the King's Road, punks now charged for their photographs to be taken. (Above) Two punks in London's Hyde Park, 26 October 1986.

Punk wurde Mitte der achtziger Jahre als heftige (und kommerzielle) Mode neu geboren. In der King's Road nahmen die Punks nun Geld, wenn sie fotografiert wurden. (Oben) Zwei Punks im Londoner Hyde Park, 26. Oktober 1986.

La renaissance du style punk dans le milieu des années 1980 fut un grand coup en termes de mode (et de sous). À King's Road, il fallait désormais payer pour photographier les punks. (Ci-dessus) Deux punks à Hyde Park, Londres, 26 octobre 1986.

The African-American 'cornrow' braided hairstyle gained fleeting popularity, thanks to Bo Derek and the 1980 film *10*.

Bo Derek machte mit ihrem Film *10–Die Traumfrau* (1980) den Afrolook mit Flechtzöpfen populär.

Le style afro-améri-cain alliant tresses et perles devint très populaire grâce à Bo Derek et le film *10* de 1980.

BERNARD GOTFRYD/HULTON|ARCHIVE

A metalhead at London's Hammersmith Odeon, 1981, the mecca for heavy metal fans in the Eighties.

Harte Mädels im Hammersmith Odeon, London, 1981, in den achtziger Jahren das Mekka der Heavy-Metal-Fans.

Tête dure dans le quartier de Hammersmith Odeon à Londres, en 1981, la Mecque des fans de heavy metal dans les années 1980.

LL Cool J says it all with beanie, dukie chain and bomber jacket at a Def Jam party, London, 1987.

LL Cool J zeigt mit Rundhut, Protzkette und Bomberjacke, wer er ist. Szene von einer Def Jam Party, London, 1987.

Tout y est avec LL Cool J, photographié lors d'une Def Jam à Londres, en 1987 : le petit bob, la chaîne en or et le blouson d'aviateur.

NORMSKI/PYMCA

Early rave fashions of 1988. The outfits are a meeting of post-Culture Club and up-and-coming Acid House.

Frühe Raver-Mode, 1988. Das Outfit ist eine Mischung von ausklingendem Culture-Club- und beginnendem Acid-House-Stil.

Précurseurs du style rave en 1988. Ces tenues sont un mélange de post-Culture Club et de pre-Acid House, laquelle était une tendance qui commençait à s'imposer.

Punk shows its
softer side with
mohair jumper and
jeans, 1986.
Knitwear made a
considerable
comeback in
the 1980s.

Mohair-Pullover
und Jeans: eine
weichere Variante
des Punk, 1986.
In den achtziger
Jahren erlebten
Strickwaren ein
modisches
Comeback.

Le style punk se fait
plus doux avec un
pull en mohair et
des jeans, 1986.
Les années 1980
furent marquées
par le grand retour
du tricot.

GAVIN WATSON/PYMCA

The dark side emerges with new variations on anti-fashion fashion. (Above) An aspiring trend-setter indulges in a do-it-yourself Mohican hair cut as part of a punk-Goth transformation.

Neue Varianten antimodischer Moden bringen die dunkle Seite nach oben. (Oben) Ein Möchtegern-Trendsetter mit selbstgemachtem Mohikanerhaarschnitt. Aus Punk wird Gothic.

Un autre versant, plus noir, apparaît avec de nouvelles variations sur le thème de la mode anti-mode. (Ci-dessus) Une débutante parmi les faiseurs de mode se fait une coupe de cheveux à la Mohican, style qui faisait partie du courant punk-gothique.

TED POLHEMUS/PYMCA

An end to such old-fashioned concerns as 'are my seams straight?' and 'does my bum look big in this?'. Flesh bursts through the ladders that led to fashion success in the world of Goth.

„Sitzen meine Nähte gerade?" „Kommt mein Hintern damit nicht zu stark heraus?" Mit solchen altmodischen Sorgen war es vorbei. In der Welt des Gothic dringt das pralle Fleisch durch die Laufmaschen und sorgt für modischen Erfolg.

C'en est fini des questions comme « le fil de mes bas était-il droit ? » ou « est-ce que j'ai l'air d'avoir un gros derrière avec ça ? ». La chair apparaît à travers les trous qui lézardent les bas, faisant le succès stylistique de la faune gothique.

9. Youth
Jugend
La jeunesse

The ultimate in street smartness – against a wall of graffiti, young males gather for a breakdancing session, 1984. Athletic, dazzlingly brilliant, slightly dangerous, above all it was something that adults simply couldn't do.

Der letzte Schrei in Sachen cooles Auftreten – männliche Jugendliche bei einer Breakdance-Session vor einer Wand mit Grafitti, 1984. Athletisch, halsbrecherisch, ein bisschen gefährlich war das schon, vor allem aber konnten Erwachsene das nicht nachmachen.

Le comble du chic dans la rue – adossés à un mur couvert de graffitis, des jeunes font du smurf, 1984. Ces performances athlétiques, aussi époustouflantes que risquées, représentaient surtout quelque chose que les adultes ne pouvaient pas faire.

9. Youth
Jugend
La jeunesse

The trend towards establishing a separate youth culture that had started in the 1950s and had come on stream in the 1960s reached full flood in the 1980s. Young people had more money and fewer inhibitions. They worked hard and played hard. Perhaps the planet was in need of care and attention, but, right now, life was for the energetic and youth had enough energy to light up the world.

East and west, every major city had its club scene. Lights flashed, pills popped, liquor was consumed in enormous quantities, people collapsed, some even died, but the beat and the dance and the fun went on, wiping out the rest of the weekend but allowing those with jobs to creep back to work in the cruel light of Monday morning.

On streets where children once cavorted, youth now exhibited their skills as skateboarders, rollerbladers or breakdancers, took their ghetto-blasters for a walk, or simply passed the time. In doorways and derelict buildings, alleys and passageways, there were those who nursed their ever-dwindling stocks of drugs and wondered where the next hit was coming from.

Die Tendenz zur Herausbildung einer eigenen Jugendkultur, die in den fünfziger Jahren eingesetzt hatte und in den sechziger Jahren in Fahrt gekommen war, war in den achtziger Jahren durchgesetzt. Die jungen Leute verfügten über mehr Geld, es gab weniger Verbote. Sie arbeiteten hart und sie liebten das harte Spiel. Es mochte notwendig sein, sich um den Planeten zu sorgen und zu kümmern, aber das Leben gehörte nun einmal den Energischen, und die Jugendlichen besaßen genügend Energie, um die Welt leuchten zu lassen.

Jede größere Stadt in Ost und West hatte ihre Clubszene. Die Lichter blitzten, Pillen putschten auf, der Alkohol floss in Strömen. Manche brachen zusammen, einige starben sogar, aber der Beat, der Tanz und der Spaß gingen weiter. Der Rest des Wochenendes zählte nicht, aber wer einen Job hatte, tankte genügend auf, um im bleiernen Licht des nächsten Montagmorgens wieder zur Arbeit zu krauchen.

Auf den Straßen, wo früher die Kinder spielten, zeigten Jugendliche nun ihre Fähigkeiten als Skateboardfahrer, Rollerblader oder Breakdancer, gingen mit dem Ghettoblaster aus oder hingen einfach nur so rum. In Hauseingängen und Abrisshäusern, auf Straßen und in Durchfahrten gammelten Süchtige mit schwindendem Nachschub und fragten sich, woher sie den nächsten Schuss nehmen sollten.

La tendance à vouloir créer une culture qui soit propre aux jeunes remonte aux années cinquante. Elle prit de l'ampleur au cours des années soixante et finit par s'imposer à part entière durant les années quatre-vingt. Les jeunes avaient plus d'argent et moins d'inhibitions. Ils travaillaient dur et, pendant leurs loisirs, consommaient de tout avec excès. La planète était malade et aurait mérité que l'on s'attarde sur son cas, mais, à cette époque-là, ce qui comptait, c'était la vie et ces jeunes dotés d'une énergie qui semblait inépuisable.

D'Est en Ouest, chaque grande ville avait une vie nocturne. Les lumières flashaient, les drogues circulaient, l'alcool se buvait en grandes quantités, des jeunes perdaient connaissance tandis que d'autres y laissèrent même leur vie. Toutefois, rien ne pouvait arrêter la musique, la danse et le plaisir. Tant pis si le reste du week-end était gâché, ceux qui avaient un job reprenaient le travail le lundi matin, la gueule complètement barbouillée.

Dans les rues, autrefois remplies d'enfants en train de courir et jouer, il y avait maintenant des jeunes qui affichaient leurs talents sur des skate-boards, en rollers ou en smurfant, qui déambulaient avec de gigantesques radiocassettes portatifs sur les épaules quand ils ne s'installaient pas sur le trottoir pour passer le temps, tout simplement. Enfin, dans l'embrasure d'une porte, dans un immeuble délabré, au détour d'une petite allée ou d'un passage, on pouvait croiser des jeunes dont le seul souci était d'assurer leur dose de drogue et qui se demandaient comment se procurer leur prochain shoot.

BILL BERNSTEIN/BLACK STAR/COLORIFIC!

Dancing lay at the centre of a great deal of social life and leisure time for many young people. (Above) Dancers hit the floor at the re-opening of Studio 54 in New York City, 15 September 1981.

Für viele junge Leute war das Tanzen ein wesentlicher Teil ihrer Freizeitaktivitäten. (Oben) Volle Aktion auf dem Tanzboden bei der Wiedereröffnung des Studio 54 in New York City, 15. September 1981.

La danse était au cœur des préoccupations d'une majorité de jeunes, c'était à la fois un divertissement et un loisir. (Ci-dessus) Danseurs acharnés lors de la réouverture du Studio 54 à New York, le 15 septembre 1981.

The joys and jewels of Studio 54 are proudly displayed by a metallic painted dancer on opening night.

Da bleibt nichts verborgen. Metallisch bemalter Tänzer selbstzufrieden im Studio 54.

Les plaisirs et trésors du Studio 54 sont affichés avec fierté par un danseur enduit de peinture métallisée le soir de l'ouverture.

TOM GATES/HULTON|ARCHIVE

DAVID SWINDELLS/PYMCA

Oh, my America. Two neo-naturists take to the floor for a rave celebrating American Independence Day at Taboo, 218 East 52nd Street, New York City, 4 July 1985.

Amerika, was ist aus dir geworden. Zwei Teilnehmerinnen einer Party feiern den amerikanischen Unabhängigkeitstag auf ihre Art im Taboo an der 218 East 52nd Street, New York City, 4. Juli 1985.

Ah l'Amérique ! Deux néonaturistes envahissent la piste de danse lors d'une soirée organisée pour la fête nationale américaine au Taboo, 218 East 52nd Street, New York, le 4 juillet 1985.

Not an optical
illusion but a
performance by
David Cabaret at
Pyramid at Heaven,
London, 1987.

Keine optische
Täuschung, sondern
eine Performance
von David Cabaret
im Pyramid at
Heaven, London,
1987.

Il ne s'agit pas d'une
illusion d'optique
mais d'une perfor-
mance de David
Cabaret réalisée au
Pyramid at Heaven à
Londres, 1987.

DAVID SWINDELLS/PYMCA

Swapping the pavement for the boards.
A breakdancer gets his mind and his head in a
whirl at a New York City venue, 1987.

Mal nicht auf dem Pflaster, sondern auf dem
Parkett. Ein Breakdancer bringt bei einer
Veranstaltung in New York City Geist und
Körper in Schwung, 1987.

Passer de la rue à la piste de danse. Un smurfer
tourbillonne, la tête et l'esprit à l'envers, sur la
scène d'un club new-yorkais, 1987.

A skateboarder
takes off from the
bottom of a chute
on the south coast of
England, Southsea,
1989.

Ein Skateboard-
fahrer hebt von
der Halfpipe ab,
Southsea an der
englischen Südküste,
1989.

Un jeune en planche
à roulettes décolle
d'une piste de skate-
board sur la côte sud
de l'Angleterre,
Southsea, 1989.

BRIAN O'HALLORAN/PYMCA

Students stretch their muscles and warm up for a dance class at Flagball School of Arts, North Carolina, 1986. Six years after the Alan Parker film *Fame*, many young people still had their sights firmly set on careers in entertainment.

Aufwärm- und Streckübungen der Eleven einer Tanzklasse der Flagball School of Arts, North Carolina, 1986. Sechs Jahre nach Alan Parkers Film *Fame* strebten viele Jugendliche verbissen eine Karriere im Unterhaltungsgeschäft an.

Échauffements divers avant le début d'une classe de danse à Flagball School of Arts en Caroline du Nord, 1986. Six ans après *Fame,* le film d'Alan Parker, il y avait encore beaucoup de jeunes déterminés à faire carrière dans le monde du spectacle.

For the hip, on the hip: the ubiquitous Sony Walkman. A young Japanese woman steps out, 1982.

Ein Accessoire der Trendbewussten, überall zu finden: Auch diese junge Japanerin trägt einen Walkman von Sony, 1982.

À la mode, l'air de rien, avec sur la hanche l'inévitable walkman de Sony. Une jeune Japonaise se distingue dans la rue, 1982.

NAOKI OKAMOTO/BLACK STAR/COLORIFIC!

Music on the move, USA 1985. It lacked the portability of the Walkman, but the ghetto-blaster allowed others to share your taste in music and its young owner the chance to annoy passing fuddy-duddies.

Bewegte Musik: Zwar war der Ghettoblaster nicht so handlich wie ein Walkman, aber auch andere kamen gezwungenermaßen in den Genuss der Musik. Für manchen Jugendlichen eine gute Chance, es den Alten einmal richtig zu zeigen.

Musique en mouvement, États-Unis, 1985. La radiocassette portable n'avait pas la légèreté du walkman, mais elle permettait de partager ses goûts musicaux en public, donnant ainsi l'occasion à son jeune propriétaire d'ennuyer ceux qui n'étaient plus dans le coup.

The message of the wall reads: 'I want some drugs.' But the boy in the frame has to be content with a cigarette, an empty foil container and a dab of glue. Such was the glamour of the drug culture in the 1980s.

„Ich will Drogen", steht an der Wand. Aber der junge Mann im Bild muss sich mit einer Zigarette, einem leeren Metallbehälter und einem Klecks Klebstoff behelfen. So sah der Glanz der Drogenkultur in den achtziger Jahren aus.

Le message écrit sur le mur dit : « Je veux de la drogue ». Mais le garçon ici photographié doit se contenter d'une cigarette, d'un sachet en aluminium vide et d'un peu de colle. C'était l'envers du miroir glamour de la culture des drogues des années 1980.

CHRISTOPH LINGG/ANZENBERGER/COLORIFIC!

Panic in Needle Park? Aftermath of a heavy smack session, Alphabet City, New York. Penalties for possession and dealing were increased in the 1980s, but the scoring and the ODs continued.

Panik im Needle Park? Szenen nach heftigem Drogenkonsum, Alphabet City, New York. Die Strafen auf den Besitz und den Handel mit Drogen wurden in den achtziger Jahren erhöht, aber der Konsum und die Todesfälle durch den goldenen Schuss nahmen nicht ab.

Panique à Needle Park ? Non, conséquences d'une sérieuse dose de smacks à Alphabet City dans l'État de New York. Les condamnations pour possession et commerce de drogues augmentèrent dans les années 1980, sans pour autant freiner la consommation et les morts par overdose.

GABE KIRCHHEIMER/BLACK STAR/COLORIFIC!

It started as a revival of the spirit of Woodstock, but the first Rainbow Gatherings of the 1980s soon developed into a world-wide movement, with camps in Europe as well as on the Washington–Oregon border, 1989 (above).

Sie begannen als eine Art Revival von Woodstock. Aus den ersten „Rainbow"-Zusammenkünften in den achtziger Jahren erwuchs eine weltweite Bewegung, die überall Großversammlungen abhielt, nicht nur in Europa, sondern auch hier, irgendwo an der Grenze zwischen den Bundesstaaten Washington und Oregon, 1989 (oben).

Rappelant l'esprit de Woodstock, les premiers rassemblements du Rainbow (mouvement Arc-en-ciel) des années 1980 devinrent très vite un phénomène mondial avec la création de camps en Europe et aux États-Unis, notamment à la frontière des États de Washington et de l'Oregon, 1989 (ci-dessus).

A scene of domestic
tranquillity inside
one of the tents at
the same Rainbow
Gathering,
Washington–Oregon,
USA, 1989.

Im Zelt geht es
häuslich-friedlich zu:
Szene von dem
gleichen „Rainbow"-
Treffen an der
Grenze zwischen
Washington und
Oregon, USA, 1989.

Scène de vie paisible
à l'intérieur d'une
tente d'un camp
du mouvement
Arc-en-ciel, aux
frontières des États
du Washington et de
l'Oregon, États-Unis,
1989.

GABE KIRCHHEIMER/BLACK STAR/COLORIFIC!

Drop 'em, boys –
lads show their
credentials at 'Disco-
Teque' in the spring
of 1988.

Lasst die Hüllen
fallen – junge Kerle
zeigen im „Disco-
Teque", was sie
haben, Frühjahr
1988.

À poil, les gars – ces
jeunes gens dévoi-
lent leurs atouts au
« Disco-Teque »,
printemps 1988.

DAVID SWINDELLS/PYMCA

DAVID SWINDELLS/PYMCA

Not quite slaves to the rave. By the late Eighties the 'lad culture' had infiltrated the scene and started to transform it. It wasn't a pretty sight. (Above) Spectrum, 1989.

Nicht nur dem Rave hörig. In den späten achtziger Jahren drang die „lad-culture", die „Saufkultur", in die Szene ein und veränderte sie. Ein erfreulicher Anblick war das nicht (oben), Spectrum, 1989.

Semi-esclaves des raves. Vers la fin des années 1980, apparut le cock-tail « mecs macho, bière et foot », en réponse aux années féministes. Ce n'était pas joli à voir. (Ci-dessus) En voici un échantillon, 1989.

When Ibiza was just another island... A drunken British tourist dead to the world outside a burger bar, 4 September 1984.

Ibiza ist auch nur eine Insel ... Abgefüllter britischer Tourist, der keinen Wunsch mehr offen hat, vor einem Imbiss, 4. September 1984.

Quand Ibiza devient un deuxième Royaume-Uni ... Un touriste britannique, ivre mort, allongé devant un bar, 4 septembre 1984.

JOHN REARDON/THE OBSERVER/HULTON|ARCHIVE

Riding the rave.
Dancers work up
a heavy sweat at
Pacha I, Ibiza, 1989.
By now the rave
scene was a part of
the island's culture.

Im Rausch des Rave.
Die Tänzer bei
ihrem schweißigen
Treiben im Pacha I,
Ibiza, 1989. Damals
war die Raverszene
schon ein Teil der
Inselkultur.

Frénésie. Danseurs
dégoulinant de sueur
au Pacha I à Ibiza,
1989. Le milieu des
discothèques et
autres clubs faisait
désormais partie de
la vie de l'île.

DAVID SWINDELLS/PYMCA

City of London policemen question a would-be anarchist near the Stock Exchange, 27 September 1984. A 'Stop the City' demonstration was expected.

Londoner Bobbys filzen einen Möchtegern-Anarchisten in der Nähe der Börse, 27. September 1984. Eine Demonstration, die die Stadt lahm legen sollte, stand ins Haus.

Des policiers de la City de Londres interrogent un pseudo-anarchiste près de la Bourse, le 27 septembre 1984. Une manifestation était prévue pour réclamer l'abolition de la City.

PA

MICHAEL GREENLAR/BLACK STAR/COLORIFIC!

A boot camp guard fails to pick on someone his own size, Forsyth, Georgia, 1987.
'Boot camp' was the popular name for the unpopular alternative incarceration facilities
pioneered in the States.

Nicht ganz seine Kragenweite: Wärter eines Straflagers in Forsyth, Georgia, hat einem
Insassen etwas mitzuteilen, 1987. „Boot Camps" hießen die Straflager, die als gar nicht
populäre Alternative zu Jugendgefängnissen in den Vereinigten Staaten eingeführt wurden.

Un gardien d'une maison d'arrêt pour adolescents s'en prend à plus petit que lui, Forsyth,
Géorgie, 1987. Surnommées « boot camps », ces maisons d'arrêt de triste réputation étaient
censées offrir une solution au problème de l'incarcération des jeunes aux États-Unis.

Life became more complicated for professional and amateur sociologists in the 1980s. In the old days, skinheads (above) were almost unanimously condemned as brutish, neo-Fascists. By 1989 'skinhead' was a style, not a personality.

Für Soziologen und solche, die sich dafür hielten, wurden die Verhältnisse in den achtziger Jahren unübersichtlicher. Früher galten Skinheads (oben) fast durchgängig als neofaschistische Schläger. Doch 1989 war das Skinhead-Auftreten eher Stil als Ausdruck einer politischen Gesinnung.

Les sociologues, professionnels ou amateurs, avaient de plus en plus de difficultés à analyser la vie quotidienne. Jusque-là, les « skinheads » (ci-dessus) étaient unanimement considérés comme des brutes néofascistes. En 1989, « skinhead » correspondait à un style et plus à une appartenance politique.

For some, however, the old ways remained. (Right) A skinhead at a British Movement rally, Notting Hill, London, 2 June 1980.

Das galt aber nicht für alle Skinheads. (Rechts) Fascho-Glatze bei einer Demonstration des nazistischen British Movement im Londoner Stadtteil Notting Hill, 2. Juni 1980.

Certains, par contre, continuèrent d'adhérer aux principes d'origine. (À droite) Skinhead à une manifestation de l'extrême-droite britannique à Notting Hill, Londres, le 2 juin 1980.

STUART NICOL/EVENING STANDARD/HULTON|ARCHIVE

10. Sport
Sport
Le sport

Ben Johnson slips into the lead during the men's 100 metres final at the Seoul Olympics, 1988. Johnson finished first, but was stripped of his gold medal two days later for using an illegal substance.

Ben Johnson geht beim 100-Meter-Lauf der Olympischen Spiele von Seoul, 1988, in Führung. Johnson ging als erster durchs Ziel, musste aber zwei Tage später seine Goldmedaille zurückgeben, weil nachgewiesen wurde, dass er gedopt war.

Ben Johnson prend la tête de la finale du 100 mètres hommes aux Jeux olympiques de Séoul, 1988. Johnson termina premier, mais fut dépouillé de sa médaille d'or deux jours plus tard pour usage de substances illicites.

10. Sport
Sport
Le sport

Never before had sport attracted so many followers, received so much publicity or generated so much wealth. Nor had it ever experienced such tragedy and drama as it did in the 1980s. Almost a hundred years earlier, the Baron de Coubertin had inaugurated the modern Olympic movement and stated the Olympic ideal. In the 1988 Olympics at Seoul what mattered was not taking illegal substances. Drugs cost Ben Johnson of Canada a gold medal; they later cost several athletes their careers.

Football was hit by appalling tragedies. In May 1985, fifty-six football fans were killed in a fire. Less than three weeks later thirty-nine fans were crushed to death in the crumbling Heysel Stadium, Brussels. Worse followed. On 15 April 1989, ninety-five Liverpool fans died during an FA Cup semi-final.

But sport continued on its way. France, West Germany and Argentina dominated international football. The USA and the Soviet Union swept the field in athletics. West Germany grabbed tennis glory through Boris Becker and Steffi Graf. India and Australia took cricket's World Cup. There was something for everyone.

Niemals zuvor besaß der Sport so viele Anhänger, niemals zuvor stand er so stark im Blickpunkt der Medien, und niemals zuvor wurde so viel Geld mit Sport verdient. Niemals zuvor aber gab es auch so viele Tragödien und Dramen im Sport. Fast 100 Jahre waren vergangen, seit Baron de Coubertin die moderne olympische Bewegung ins Leben gerufen und das olympische Ideal aufgestellt hatte. 1988, bei den Olympischen Spielen von Seoul war Doping das Thema. Der Kanadier Ben Johnson verlor seine Goldmedaille, weil er gedopt war; später mussten mehrere andere Athleten wegen Doping ihre Sportler-karriere aufgeben.

Die Welt des Fußballs wurde von schrecklichen Tragödien getroffen. Im Mai 1985 starben 56 Fußballzuschauer bei einem Brand. Kaum drei Wochen später kamen 39 Fans beim Einsturz einer Mauer im Brüsseler Heysel-Stadion zu Tode. Und Katastrophen noch größeren Ausmaßes folgten: Am 15. April 1989 starben unmittelbar vor dem Pokal-halbfinale 95 Liverpooler Fans.

Aber der Sport ging unbeirrt weiter. Frankreich, Westdeutschland und Argentinien dominierten das internationale Fußballgeschehen. In der Leichtathletik räumten die USA und die Sowjetunion ab. Westdeutschland erntete mit Boris Becker und Steffi Graf Tennisruhm. Den Weltcup im Kricket sicherten sich Indien und Australien. Für jeden gab es etwas, worüber er sich freuen konnte.

Jamais auparavant le sport n'avait attiré autant de spectateurs, fait l'objet d'autant de publicité et rapporté autant d'argent. Jamais non plus il n'avait connu autant de drames et de coups de théâtre que durant les années quatre-vingt. Un siècle plus tôt ou presque, le baron de Coubertin avait inauguré les Jeux olympiques modernes et ressuscité cet idéal sportif. Aux Jeux olympiques de Séoul en 1988, l'essentiel était ailleurs, ce qui comptait, c'était de ne pas avoir consommé de substances illicites. Le Canadien Ben Johnson fut dépouillé de sa médaille d'or pour avoir fait usage de drogues. D'autres athlètes connurent le même sort et durent renoncer à leur carrière.

D'horribles tragédies endeuillèrent le monde du football. En mai 1985, 56 supporters moururent dans un incendie. Presque trois semaines plus tard, 39 personnes furent écra-sées quand un mur du stade du Heysel s'effondra. Il y eut pire encore. Le 15 avril 1989, 95 supporters de Liverpool trouvèrent la mort pendant la Coupe de football britannique.

Le sport continua néanmoins sur sa lancée. La France, l'Allemagne de l'Ouest et l'Argentine dominèrent la scène du football international. Les États-Unis et l'Union sovié-tique raflèrent toutes les médailles en athlétisme. L'Allemagne de l'Ouest connut la gloire au tennis grâce à Boris Becker et Steffi Graf. L'Inde et l'Australie remportèrent la coupe du monde de cricket. Il y en avait pour tout le monde.

PETER GINTER/BLACK STAR/COLORIFIC!

(Opposite) Carl Lewis in the blocks at the World Championships, Rome, Italy, 1987. For much of the 1980s Lewis was the fastest man in the world. (Above) Florence Griffith Joyner stretches those muscles, 1989.

(Gegenüberliegende Seite) Carl Lewis in den Startblöcken bei der Leichtathletikwelt-meisterschaft in Rom, 1987. Fast bis zum Ende der achtziger Jahre blieb Lewis der schnellste Mann der Welt. (Oben) Florence Griffith Joyner beim Stretching, 1989.

(Ci-contre) Carl Lewis dans les starting blocks lors du championnat du monde à Rome, Italie, 1987. Lewis fut l'homme le plus rapide du monde de toute la décennie ou presque. (Ci-dessus) Florence Griffith Joyner en séance d'échauffement, 1989.

Sebastian Coe
establishes a new
world record for
the mile – 3 minutes
31.26 seconds,
Zurich,
21 August 1981.

Sebastian Coe
stellt einen neuen
Weltrekord über
die Meile auf –
3:31,26, Zürich,
21. August 1981.

Sebastian Coe
établit un nouveau
record pour le
mile, 3 minutes
31,26 secondes,
Zurich,
21 août 1981.

Steve Ovett (388) struggles in the final of the 1500 metres, Los Angeles Olympics, 1984. Cram (362) took the silver medal while Coe took the gold.

Steve Ovett (388) fightet im Finale des 1500-Meter-Laufs bei den Olympischen Spielen von Los Angeles, 1984. Es siegte Coe, Cram (362) wurde Zweiter.

Steve Ovett (388) lutte durant la finale du 1500 mètres aux Jeux olympiques de Los Angeles, 1984. Cram (362) remporta la médaille d'argent tandis que Coe décrocha la médaille d'or.

Björn Borg sinks to
his knees after
winning his fifth
successive men's
singles championship
at Wimbledon,
July 1980.

Nach seinem fünften
Sieg in Folge bei den
Tennismeisterschaften
von Wimbledon sinkt
Björn Borg auf die
Knie, Juli 1980.

Björn Borg tombe à
genoux après avoir
remporté le tournoi
de Wimbledon
pour la cinquième
fois consécutive,
juillet 1980.

John McEnroe in a pit of despair after losing a point in the Wimbledon Championships, July 1989. His days of triumph in the early 1980s were over. There were new stars abroad.

John McEnroe verzweifelt, wieder ein Punkt verloren. Szene aus Wimbledon, Juli 1989. McEnroe hatte seine Glanzzeit in den frühen achtziger Jahren, aber nun standen neue Stars an der Spitze.

Geste de désespoir pour John McEnroe qui vient de perdre un point à Wimbledon, juillet 1989. Ses jours de gloire du début des années 1980 étaient terminés. De nouvelles vedettes apparaissaient à l'horizon.

Boris Becker at full stretch during the French Open Championships, Paris, 1987. It was a lean year for Becker.

Boris Becker macht sich lang: Szene von den French Open in Paris, 1987. Es war ein mageres Jahr für den deutschen Tennisstar.

Boris Becker tendu comme un élastique à Roland-Garros, Paris, en 1987, qui fut une année morose pour lui.

Forehand. Steffi
Graf on her way
to winning the
Australian Open,
Melbourne,
January 1989.

Vorhand. Steffi Graf
auf dem Weg zum
Sieg bei den offenen
australischen
Meisterschaften
in Melbourne,
Januar 1989.

Coup droit. Steffi
Graf sur le point de
remporter l'Open
d'Australie,
Melbourne,
janvier 1989.

CLIVE BRUNSKILL/ALLSPORT

Backhand? Ivan
Lendl, Wimbledon,
July 1989, the year in
which he also won
the Australian Open
for the first time.

Rückhand? Ivan
Lendl in Wimbledon,
Juli 1989.
Im gleichen Jahr
gewann er zum ersten
Mal die australischen
Meisterschaften.

Revers ? Ivan Lendl
à Wimbledon en
juillet 1989, l'année
où il gagna pour
la première fois
l'open d'Australie.

Leon Spinks,
Heavyweight
Champion of
the World, picks
on a flyweight,
Miami Airport,
18 April 1988.

Leon Spinks,
Weltmeister im
Schwergewicht,
krallt sich auf
dem Flughafen
von Miami ein
Fliegengewicht,
18. April 1988.

Leon Spinks,
champion du
monde des poids
lourds, soulève un
poids mouche,
aéroport de Miami,
18 avril 1988.

TIM CHAPMAN/LIAISON AGENCY

Mike Tyson with promoter Don King (in private breeze), 1988. These were the glory years for 'Iron Mike', who had world title wins over James 'Bonecrusher' Smith, Tyrell Smith, Larry Holmes, Michael Spinks, Frank Bruno and Carl Williams.

Mike Tyson und Boxveranstalter Don King (mit bekannter Sturmfrisur), 1988. Das waren die besten Jahre des „Eisernen Mike"; er siegte in Titelkämpfen gegen James „Bonecrusher" Smith, Tyrell Smith, Larry Holmes, Michael Spinks, Frank Bruno und Carl Williams.

Mike Tyson et son promoteur Don King (cheveux en l'air), 1988. Ce furent les années glorieuses de « Iron Mike » qui remporta les titres de champion du monde face à James « Bonecrusher » Smith, Tyrell Smith, Larry Holmes, Michael Spinks, Frank Bruno et Carl Williams.

First round KO. Mike Tyson is restrained by the referee after putting Michael Spinks on the canvas, Atlantic City, 27 June 1988.

Knockout in der ersten Runde. Mit Mühe kann der Ringrichter Mike Tyson bändigen, der gerade Michael Spinks auf die Bretter geschickt hat. Atlantic City, 27. Juni 1988.

K.O. au premier round. L'arbitre retient Mike Tyson qui vient de mettre Michael Spinks au tapis, Atlantic City, en juin 1988.

You lookin' at me?
Mike Tyson poses
during training in
January 1986.
Training was his
least favourite part
of the fight game.

Was guckst du so?
Mike Tyson posiert
während eines
Trainings im Januar
1986. Das Trainieren
war der Teil des
Kampfsports, den er
überhaupt nicht
mochte.

C'est moi que vous
regardez ? Mike
Tyson pose pour les
photographes
durant une séance
d'entraînement en
janvier 1986. L'en-
traînement était ce
qu'il aimait le
moins ; il préférait
le combat.

ROBERT DIBUE/ALLSPORT

In the bank. US
basketball star
Michael Jordan
in his classic 'Air
Jordan' leap for a
Nike advertisement,
1987.

Und rein damit.
Basketballstar
Michael Jordan bei
seinem berühmten
Luftsprung, mit dem
er für Nike Reklame
machte, 1987.

Dans le filet.
Michael Jordan, la
star américaine du
basket, accomplit
son grand classique,
le fameux saut de
« Air Jordan », pour
une publicité de
Nike, en 1987.

In the basket. Magic Johnson of the Los Angeles Lakers goes for a basket during the 1989 championships.

Und rein in den Korb. Magic Johnson von den Los Angeles Lakers schickt sich bei den Meisterschaften von 1989 an, einen Korb zu erzielen.

Dans la corbeille. Magic Johnson des Los Angeles Lakers sur le point de marquer durant le championnat de 1989.

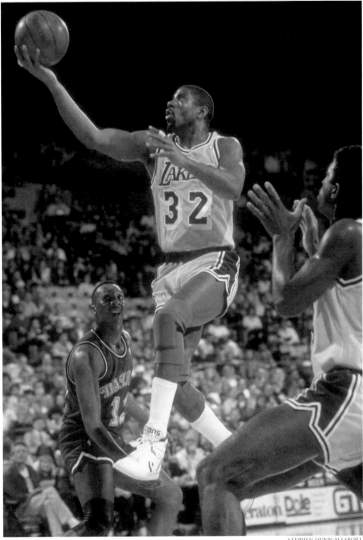

Beam me up,
Stocky. Chelle Stock
of the USA at the
women's team
gymnastics final,
Seoul Olympics,
21 September 1988.

Beam' mich rauf,
Stocky. Chelle Stock,
USA, im Mann-
schaftsfinale des
Frauenturnens bei
den Olympischen
Spielen von Seoul,
21. September 1988.

Allez, un petit
sourire ! L'Améri-
caine Chelle Stock
lors de la finale
femmes de gymnas-
tique aux Jeux olym-
piques de Séoul,
21 septembre 1988.

Another perfect 10?
Nadia Comaneci of
Romania on her way
to gold at the
Moscow Olympics,
19 July 1980, the
year she excelled.

Wieder eine 10?
Die Rumänin Nadia
Comaneci auf ihrem
Weg zur Gold-
medaille bei den
Olympischen Spie-
len in Moskau,
19. Juli 1980. Ein
Jahr des Triumphs
für die Turnerin.

Encore un 10 ?
La Roumaine Nadia
Comaneci sur le
chemin de l'or aux
Jeux olympiques
de Moscou,
le 19 juillet 1980,
année durant
laquelle elle excella.

TONY DUFFY/ALLSPORT

MIKE POWELL/ALLSPORT

Horses and riders clear not the highest but perhaps the hardest jump in the Grand National – Becher's Brook, Aintree, Liverpool, April 1983. It was originally a water jump, named after Captain Martin Becher.

Reiter und Pferde stellen sich dem zwar nicht höchsten, aber schwierigsten Hindernis beim Grand National, dem Becher's Brook, Aintree, Liverpool, April 1983. Ursprünglich war das nach Captain Martin Becher benannte Hindernis ein Wassergraben.

Chevaux et jockeys franchissent non pas l'obstacle le plus haut mais le plus difficile du prix du Grand National, le Becher's Brook, Aintree, Liverpool, avril 1983. À l'origine, c'était un brook, qui fut ainsi nommé en souvenir du capitaine Martin Becher.

Captain Becher took a tumble from his horse, Conrad, in 1839. (Above) Riders and horses (including the grey Dark Ivy, centre) follow in the captain's footsteps during the 1987 Grand National.

Captain Becher fiel 1839 von seinem Pferd Conrad. (Oben) Auch beim Grand National von 1987 wandelten Reiter und Pferde (in der Mitte der Grauschimmel Dark Ivy) auf Bechers Spuren.

C'est ici que le capitaine Becher tomba avec son cheval Conrad en 1839. (Ci-dessus) Chevaux et jockeys (y compris le cheval gris Dark Ivy, au centre) sur les traces du capitaine durant le prix du Grand National de 1987.

Mauricio Gugelmin of Brazil takes to the air
after shunting Nigel Mansell's Ferrari during
the French Grand Prix, 9 July 1989.

Der Brasilianer Mauricio Gugelmin hebt ab,
nachdem er Nigel Mansells Ferrari beim
französischen Grand Prix beseite geschoben
hatte, 9. Juli 1989.

Le Brésilien Mauricio Gugelmin s'envole
dans les airs après avoir percuté la Ferrari de
Nigel Mansell durant le Grand Prix de
France, 9 juillet 1989.

DAVID CANNON/ALLSPORT

French captain Michel Platini wheels away in triumph after his goal against
Brazil in the World Cup quarter-final at the Jalisco Stadium, Guadalajara,
Mexico, 21 June 1986. France won 4-3 on penalties.

Ein jubelnder Michel Platini, Kapitän der französischen Nationalmannschaft,
nach seinem Tor im Viertelfinale der Weltmeisterschaft im Jalisco-Stadion,
Guadalajara, Mexiko, 21. Juni 1986. Frankreich siegte gegen Brasilien mit 4:3
im Elfmeterschießen.

Le capitaine français, Michel Platini, rayonnant de joie après avoir marqué un
but contre le Brésil en quart de finale de la Coupe du monde au Stade de Jalisco,
Guadalajara, Mexique, 21 juin 1986. La France gagna aux penalties 4 à 3.

ALLSPORT UK

Ruud Gullit (left) and Gerald Vanenburg take off on a lap of honour
after Holland beat the Soviet Union 2-0 in the European
Championship Final, Olympic Stadium, Munich, 25 June 1988.

Ruud Gullit (links) und Gerald Vanenburg drehen nach dem 2:0-Sieg
der Niederlande über die Sowjetunion im Finale der Europameister-
schaft eine Ehrenrunde, Olympiastadion, München, 25. Juni 1988.

Ruud Gullit (à gauche) et Gerald Vanenburg font un tour d'honneur
après la victoire de la Hollande sur l'Union soviétique lors de la
finale du championnat européen au Stade olympique de Munich,
le 25 juin 1988.

ALLSPORT UK

The camera cannot lie; the ref couldn't see. Diego Maradona and the Hand of God slip the ball past Peter Shilton, World Cup quarter-final, Mexico City, 22 June 1986. English hearts were broken.

Die Kamera lügt nicht, aber der Schiedsrichter hat es nicht gesehen. Diego Maradona lupft im Viertelfinale der Weltmeisterschaft in Mexiko-Stadt mit goldenem Händchen den Ball über Peter Shilton, 22. Juni 1986. Ein furchtbarer Schlag für die englischen Fans.

La caméra ne ment pas, mais l'arbitre n'avait pas pu voir le geste. La « main de Dieu » de Diego Maradona pousse la balle devant Peter Shilton durant le match des quarts de finale de la Coupe du monde, Mexico, 22 juin 1986. Les Anglais en eurent le cœur brisé.

Three weeks earlier, the Knees of God were most cruelly fouled. Maradona in an earlier World Cup game, June 1986.

Drei Wochen zuvor musste aber auch Maradona leiden. Heftiges Foul gegen den argentinischen Star bei einem früheren Welt-meisterschaftsspiel, Juni 1986.

Trois semaines plus tôt, les genoux du « Dieu » furent cruellement percu-tés. Maradona photographié pendant un des premiers matchs de la Coupe du monde, en juin 1986.

EAMONN McCABE/THE OBSERVER/HULTON|ARCHIVE

One of the darkest days in the history of sport: football fans are crushed after
a wall collapses at the Heysel Stadium, Brussels, 29 May 1985, just before the
start of the European Cup Final.

Eine der schwärzesten Stunden in der Geschichte des Sports: Fußballfans wurden niedergetrampelt, nachdem kurz vor Beginn des Europacup-Finales eine
Mauer im Brüsseler Heysel-Stadion zusammengebrochen war, 29. Mai 1985.

Un des jours les plus sombres de l'histoire du sport : des supporters sont
écrasés suite à l'effondrement d'un mur du stade du Heysel à Bruxelles
le 29 mai 1985, peu avant le début de la finale de la Coupe d'Europe.

NICK DIDLICK/REUTERS/HULTON|ARCHIVE

Trouble began when fighting broke out between supporters of Liverpool and Juventus. By the time it was over, thirty-nine lay dead and more than 400 injured. (Above) A harrowing image of the aftermath.

Das Unheil begann, als Schlägereien zwischen den Fans des FC Liverpool und Juventus Turin ausbrachen. Als alles vorbei war, waren 39 Tote und mehr als 400 Verletzte zu beklagen. (Oben) Danach, Szenen des Schreckens.

Tout commença lorsque des bagarres éclatèrent entre supporters de Liverpool et de la Juventus. Quand le calme revint, on dénombra 39 corps sans vie et plus de 400 blessés. (Ci-dessus) Image déchirante de la tragédie.

11. Children
Kinder
Les enfants

Two young children photographed in south-west China, 1989. Whatever benefits it had brought, forty years of Communism had apparently failed to alter traditional gender stereotyping.

Ein kleiner Junge und ein kleines Mädchen im Südwesten Chinas, 1989. Was auch immer die Ergebnisse von 40 Jahren kommunistischer Herrschaft sein mochten, an den traditionellen Geschlechterrollen hatte sich offensichtlich nichts geändert.

Petit couple d'enfants photographiés dans le sud-ouest de la Chine, 1989. Peu importe les avantages du régime, quarante ans de communisme n'ont pas suffi à mettre un terme à la répartition traditionnelle des rôles.

11. Children
   Kinder
   Les enfants

The 1960s had invented the teenager; the 1970s had seen the full flowering of 'youth'. It was time for children to reappear on the world stage. In the 1980s they did so in a series of tragedies whose themes were war, famine and exploitation. One 14-year-old from Mozambique declared: 'I have never seen peace. I don't know what peace is. I have never lived in freedom.' He spoke for millions of African children.

All over the world there were stories of gangs of children who lived by begging on the streets, stealing the hubcaps of cars, prostituting themselves, scrabbling for food on garbage heaps. Television viewers flinched as they saw how children lived in the Sudan, in Beirut, in Romanian orphanages, in military camps, in the slums of South America.

In more comfortable lands, traders set out their stalls for children. There was a spate of children's films, from *ET* to *Flash Gordon* and *Superman*. Toyshops bulged with a mixture of the old hand-made toys and new big money-spinners that were battery operated and made of plastic; bookshops were filled with 'game books', fantasy adventure stories. But the most popular new toy was the computer.

Die sechziger Jahre brachten den „Teenager" hervor, in den siebzigern sprach man von den „Jugendlichen". Es war an der Zeit, dass die Kinder auf die Bühne der Welt zurückkehrten. In den achtziger Jahren waren sie auf schreckliche Weise wieder an der Reihe – im Zusammenhang mit Krieg, Hunger und Ausbeutung. Ein 14-jähriger Junge aus Mosambik erklärte: „Ich habe niemals Frieden erlebt. Ich weiß gar nicht, was Frieden ist. Freiheit habe ich nie kennen gelernt." Er sprach für Millionen afrikanischer Kinder.

Aus aller Welt wurde von Kinderbanden berichtet, die auf den Straßen bettelten, Radkappen stahlen, sich prostituierten, Müllhalden nach Essbarem durchstöberten.

Die Fernsehzuschauer erschraken über die Bilder, die die Lebensbedingungen von Kindern im Sudan, in Beirut, in rumänischen Waisenhäusern, in Militärcamps oder den Slums Südamerikas dokumentierten.

In den wohlhabenden Ländern ging hingegen die Wirtschaft auf Kinderfang. Auf Kinder zugeschnittene Filme hatten Hochkonjunktur, *E.T.*, *Flash Gordon* oder *Superman*. Die Spielzeugläden barsten vor Angeboten. Neben den traditionellen, handgefertigten Dingen gab es als neue Kassenschlager batteriebetriebene Geräte aus Plastik; es gab auch Bücher zum Spielen mit Fantasyinhalten. Doch das beliebteste neue Spielzeug war zweifellos der Computer.

Les années soixante avaient inventé l'adolescent et les années soixante-dix avaient assisté à l'épanouissement de cette « jeunesse ». Il était temps que les enfants réoccupent le devant de la scène mondiale. C'est ce qui leur arriva dans les années quatre-vingt, mais à travers une série de tragédies nommées guerre, famine et exploitation. Un gamin de 14 ans du Mozambique déclara : « Je n'ai jamais connu la paix. Je ne sais pas ce que c'est. Je n'ai jamais vécu libre. » Ce qu'il disait, des millions d'autres enfants africains auraient pu le dire à sa place.

Partout dans le monde, il y avait des bandes d'enfants qui survivaient en mendiant dans les rues, en volant des enjoliveurs, en se prostituant, en cherchant de la nourriture parmi des montagnes de déchets. Les téléspectateurs tressaillaient quand ils voyaient comment les enfants vivaient au Soudan, à Beyrouth, dans les orphelinats roumains, dans les camps militaires ou dans les bidonvilles d'Amérique latine.

Dans les pays riches, tout était bon pour séduire les enfants. Le cinéma se mit à produire une série de films pour enfants, allant de *E.T.* à *Flash Gordon* et *Superman*. Les magasins de jouets regorgeaient de jouets classiques faits main et de nouvelles inventions en plastique qui fonctionnaient avec des batteries et qui étaient de vraies mines. Les librairies étaient remplies de livres-jeux, d'aventures fantastiques. Mais ce fut l'ordinateur qui devint le plus populaire des jouets.

The hug of humanity. Pope John Paul II embraces a child AIDS victim, 1987. The picture helped de-stigmatise sufferers from the disease.

Eine Umarmung für die Menschlichkeit. Papst Johannes Paul II. umarmt ein Kind, das Träger des HIV-Virus ist, 1987. Dieses Bild half bei dem Kampf gegen die Ausgrenzung der Aidskranken.

Geste d'humanité. Le pape Jean-Paul II embrasse un enfant victime du sida, 1987. Cette photographie permit de dé-stigmatiser les victimes de cette maladie.

Just say no. Nancy
Reagan, First Lady
of the United States,
at an anti-drugs
demonstration,
Washington, DC,
May 1988.

Sag einfach nein.
Nancy Reagan, die
amerikanische First
Lady, bei einer Anti-
Drogen-Veranstal-
tung in Washington,
D. C., Mai 1988.

« Dis non, c'est tout ».
Nancy Reagan, la
première dame des
États-Unis, lors d'une
manifestation anti-
drogue, Washington,
mai 1998.

Francie, a 13-year-old suffering from Hutchinson-Gilford syndrome, April 1986. The condition leads to premature ageing, which affects the heart and arteries. Few victims survive beyond the age of 30.

Francie, 13 Jahre alt, leidet an dem Hutchinson-Gilford-Syndrom, das vorzeitige Alterungsprozesse auslöst, die Herz und Arterien betreffen, April 1986. Nur wenige Kranke erreichen das 30. Lebensjahr.

Francie, âgé de 13 ans, atteint du syndrome de Hutchinson-Gilford, avril 1986. Cette maladie entraîne un vieillissement prématuré, affectant le cœur et les artères. Rares sont les victimes qui franchissent le cap des 30 ans.

Isolated from germs, 6-year-old David undergoes tests at the clinical research centre of the Texas Children's Hospital, September 1980. David was a victim of severe combined immune deficiency, a hereditary disease affecting only males.

Vor Keimen geschützt. Der sechsjährige David bei Tests im klinischen Forschungszentrum des Texas Children's Hospital, September 1980. David litt unter schwerer kombinierter Immunschwäche, einer Erbkrankheit, an der nur Jungen erkranken können.

Isolé des microbes, David, âgé de 6 ans, subit des tests au centre de recherches cliniques de l'hôpital des enfants du Texas, septembre 1980. David souffre d'une grave déficience du système immunitaire, une maladie héréditaire qui ne touche que les garçons.

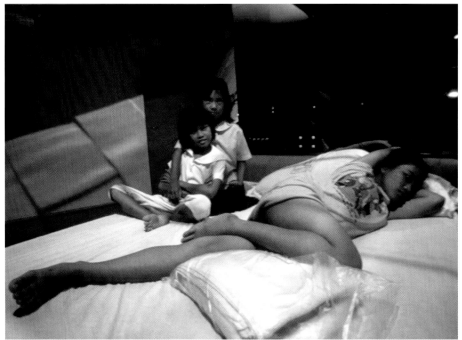

CHRISTOPH HENNING/FOTOARCHIV/COLORIFIC!

A brief respite from work, a moment back in childhood. Child prostitutes at the
Queensland Lodge, Manila, the Philippines, 1989. Such abuse was centuries old.
The awakening of the world's conscience was a new phenomenon.

Ein kurzer Augenblick des Ausruhens, für einen kurzen Moment zurück in die
Kindheit. Kinder, die als Prostituierte arbeiten, in der Queensland Lodge in Manila,
Philippinen, 1989. Missbrauch dieser Art gab es schon seit Jahrhunderten, doch
nun regte sich das Weltgewissen.

Bref répit après le travail, un retour en enfance. Des enfants prostitués au Queensland Lodge à Manille, Philippines, 1989. Ces abus duraient depuis des siècles, le
fait que le monde en prenne conscience était par contre un phénomène nouveau.

Thai bar girls compete in a condom-blowing contest as part of the Thailand Fights AIDS campaign held in the red light district of Bangkok, 6 September 1989. One of the signs reads: 'We need your help & co-operation.' Not enough has arrived – yet.

Thailändische Barfrauen bei einem Wettbewerb im Kondomaufblasen, der Teil einer thailändischen Anti-Aids-Kampagne im Rotlichtbezirk von Bangkok war, 6. September 1989. Auf einem der Plakate heißt es: „Wir brauchen eure Hilfe & Zusammenarbeit". Bis heute ist nicht genügend Hilfe eingetroffen.

Des employées de bar thaïlandaises participent au concours des préservatifs-ballons qui fait partie d'une campagne intitulée « La Thaïlande lutte contre le sida » et qui est organisée dans les quartiers chauds de Bangkok, 6 septembre 1989. Une pancarte dit : « Nous avons besoin de votre aide et de votre collaboration ». À ce jour, il reste encore beaucoup à faire.

Other distractions. Palestinian school-girls file past Israeli soldiers who are frisking adult Palestinians on the Gaza Strip, November 1986.

Angst. Palästinen-sische Schulmädchen müssen an israeli-schen Soldaten vorbei, die gerade erwachsene Palästi-nenser filzen, Gazastreifen, November 1986.

Autres distractions. Des petites Palesti-niennes passent devant des soldats israéliens qui fouillent des Palestiniens dans la bande de Gaza, novembre 1986.

Life returns to normality on the streets of El Salvador, Central America, 1982. A troop of guerrilla fighters had just passed through the town of Sanbertoco when these children set off for school.

In die Straßen des mittelamerikanischen Staats El Salvador kehrt die Normalität zurück, 1982. Nachdem gerade ein Trupp von Guerilleros durch die Stadt Sanbertoco gezogen ist, gehen diese Kinder zur Schule.

La vie reprend son cours normal dans les rues du Salvador, Amérique centrale, 1982. Ces enfants partaient pour l'école quand une bande de guérilleros traversa la ville de Sanbertoco.

Children take to the streets of Beirut at the height of the fighting, March 1985. There were plenty of 12-year-old soldiers in the Lebanon at this time, with 'heavy-duty lace-up boots, skinhead haircuts and Kalashnikovs', reported one surgeon.

Mädchen als Kämpfer in den Straßen Beiruts auf dem Höhepunkt der Gefechte um die Stadt, März 1985. Viele 12-Jährige dienten zu dieser Zeit im Libanon als Soldaten, Kinder „kahl geschoren, mit schweren Schnürstiefeln und Kalaschnikows", berichtete ein Arzt.

Les enfants descendent dans les rues de Beyrouth au plus fort des combats, mars 1985. À cette époque, il n'était pas rare de voir des enfants-soldats de 12 ans équipés de «bottes montantes, de coupes de cheveux style skinhead et de Kalashnikovs» témoigna un chirurgien.

A young recruit to the Ku Klux Klan gives a Nazi salute. In some places old obscenities lingered on into the 1980s.

Junger Rekrut des Ku-Klux-Clan beim Nazigruß. In manchen Gegenden lebten alte Obszönitäten auch in den achtziger Jahren weiter.

Jeune recrue du Ku Klux Klan effectuant le salut nazi. Les années 1980 ne furent pas épargnées par des gestes obscènes datant d'une autre époque et exécutés en certains lieux.

In a world of his own, a boy patrols the outskirts of West Wycombe, Buckinghamshire, keeping it safe for democracy, 1981. Happily, the weapon is a toy and nothing worse than unemployment threatened his town.

In seiner eigenen Welt geht dieser Junge am Stadtrand von West Wycombe, Buckinghamshire, England, auf Streife und sichert die Demokratie, 1981. Glücklicherweise handelt es sich um ein Spielzeuggewehr – seine Stadt ist schlimmstenfalls von Arbeitslosigkeit bedroht.

Dans son monde à lui. Ce garçon patrouille pour faire respecter la démocratie dans les environs de West Wycombe, Buckinghamshire, 1981. Heureusement, l'arme n'est qu'un jouet et seul le chômage représentait une menace pour sa ville.

The greatest craze of the 1980s. A young skateboarder, wisely wearing helmet, and elbow and knee pads (don't leave home without them), displays concentration and balance, May 1981.

Der stärkste Kick der achtziger Jahre. Ein junger Skateboardfahrer, richtig ausgerüstet mit Helm, Ellbogen- und Knieschützern (nie vergessen!) zeigt Konzentration und Gleichgewichtssinn, Mai 1981.

La plus grande folie des années 1980. Un garçon en skateboard, sagement équipé d'un casque, de genouillères et de protections pour les coudes (selon les recommandations sans cesse répétées des parents) fait preuve de concentration et d'équilibre, en mai 1981.

Ten-year-old Terry
O'Neill masters
Rubik's Cube at the
British Toy and
Hobby Fair, Earl's
Court, London,
2 February 1981.

Der zehnjährige
Terry O'Neill
meistert den
Zauberwürfel bei
der Britischen Spiel-
zeug- und Freizeit-
messe in Earl's
Court, London,
2. Februar 1981.

Terry O'Neill, âgé
de 10 ans, réussit à
reconstituer le cube
de Rubik pendant
la foire britannique
des jouets et des
loisirs de Earl's
Court, Londres,
le 2 février 1981.

STANLEY DEVON/KEYSTONE/HULTON|ARCHIVE

SIMON NORFOLK/PYMCA

Please sir…? A hungry pupil hopes for a second sausage in the queue for school dinners, Wales, 1989. For an increasing number of children, the school dinner was their one hot meal of the day.

Nachschlag, bitte … Eine hungrige Schülerin hofft auf ein zweites Stück Wurst an der Essensausgabe einer walisischen Schule, 1989. Für eine wachsende Zahl von Kindern war die Schulspeisung die einzige warme Mahlzeit am Tag.

S'il vous plaît, Monsieur … Une élève affamée, qui fait la queue à la cantine, espère avoir une deuxième saucisse, Pays de Galles, 1989. Il y avait toujours plus d'enfants pour qui le déjeuner à l'école constituait le seul repas chaud de la journée.

A boy helps himself at a soup kitchen, New York City, September 1989. Research into child health revealed that malnutrition was not confined to the Third World in the 1980s.

Selbstbedienung in einer Suppenküche in New York City, September 1989. Untersuchungen zur Gesundheit von Kindern erbrachten, dass Unterernährung in den achtziger Jahren keineswegs nur ein Problem der Dritten Welt war.

Un garçon se sert de soupe, New York, septembre 1989. Des recherches menées sur la santé infantile démontrèrent que, dans les années 1980, la malnutrition ne concernait pas seulement les pays du tiers-monde.

MARK PERLSTEIN/BLACK STAR/COLORIFIC!

The delights of the VDU. For many children the computer was a
modern magic lantern, opening up new worlds, revealing new
wonders and ultimately leading to new employment opportunities.

Die Zauberwelt des Bildschirms. Für viele Kinder wurde der Computer
zur modernen Laterna Magica, die neue Welten eröffnete, neue Wunder
enthüllte und letztlich auch neue Beschäftigungschancen bot.

La magie de l'écran. Pour beaucoup d'enfants, l'ordinateur devint la
lanterne magique des temps modernes, celle qui permettait de découvrir
des mondes nouveaux tout en dévoilant de nouvelles merveilles et qui,
plus tard, offrirait de nouveaux débouchés professionnels.

SIMONA CALI COCUZZA/BLACK STAR/COLORIFIC!

For others, computers were thousands of miles and millions of pesos away. A young coal vendor hugs his doll in a shanty town, somewhere in El Salvador 1988.

Für andere lagen Computer außer Reichweite. Eine junge Kohlenverkäuferin liebkost ihre Puppe in einem Slum irgendwo in El Salvador, 1988.

Pour d'autres, les ordinateurs étaient à des millions de pesos et de pesos. Dans un bidonville, quelque part au Salvador, une petite vendeuse de charbon pose avec sa poupée.

12. All human life
Menschliches, Allzumenschliches
Petits et grands événements de la vie

An AIDS victim being massaged by Irene Smith, a hospice
therapist, in San Francisco, California, 1986. Two weeks later,
the poor man died.

Irene Smith, Pflegerin in einem Hospiz in San Francisco,
Kalifornien, massiert einen Aidskranken, 1986. Der bedauerns-
werte Mann hatte nur noch zwei Wochen zu leben.

Séance de massage pour un malade du sida avec Irene Smith,
thérapeute, à San Francisco, Californie, 1986. Le pauvre homme
devait mourir deux semaines plus tard.

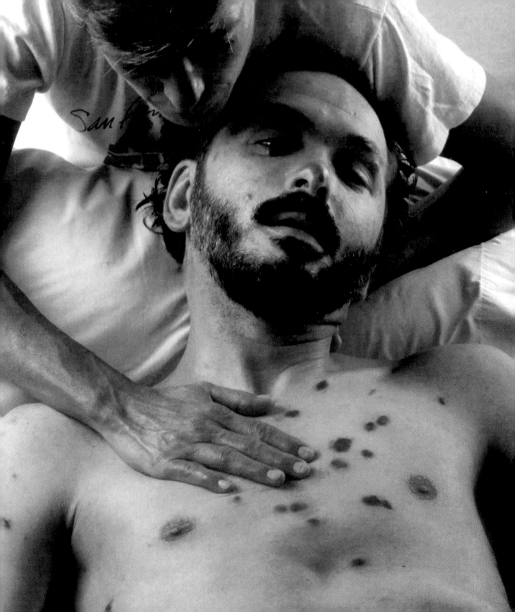

12. All human life
Menschliches, Allzumenschliches
Petits et grands événements de la vie

To and fro swung the pendulum of progress and reaction. The first black Miss America was crowned in September 1983. Just over a year later Margie Velma Barfield became the first woman to be executed in the USA for more than twenty-two years. Crack cocaine appeared. Ben and Jerry became ice-cream millionaires. After scandals involving Jimmy Swaggart ('moral transgression') and Jim Bakker (fraud), two of America's most popular TV ministers faded from the screen.

Elsewhere, the Turin Shroud was shown to have been a low-tech medieval creation, and *The Hitler Diaries* to have been the product of a fertile imagination but not that of the Führer. The matador Francisco Rivera died after being gored in the thigh: the offending bull's mother was promptly killed. In England the Yorkshire Ripper was convicted of murdering thirteen women.

More people married, more divorced. There were more holidays. For the fortunate minority, the world opened up like a giant playground. For the majority, there were brief respites from want and misery, when hope bloomed like a flower in the desert.

Das Pendel von Fortschritt und Rückschritt schlug in beide Richtungen aus. Die erste afroamerikanische Miss America wurde im September 1983 gekürt. Nur ein Jahr später wurde Margie Velma Barfield in den USA als erste Frau seit mehr als 22 Jahren hingerichtet. Crack erschien in der Drogenszene. Ben und Jerry wurden Eiskrem-Millionäre. Nach Skandalen und Anklagen verschwanden mit Jimmy Swaggart („unmoralisches Verhalten") und Jim Bakker (Betrug) zwei der populärsten amerikanischen Fernsehprediger vom Bildschirm.

In anderen Ländern erwiesen sich das Turiner Grabtuch als eine mit einfachen technischen Mitteln hergestellte Schöpfung des Mittelalters und die Hitler-Tagebücher als einer lebhaften Phantasie, doch nicht der des „Führers" entsprungen. Der Matador Francisco Rivera starb an der Verletzung, die ihm ein Stier zufügte: Die Kuh, die den Stier geboren hatte, wurde auf der Stelle getötet. In England wurde der Yorkshire Ripper des Mordes an 13 Frauen überführt.

Die Zahl der Ehen und Scheidungen nahm zu. Es gab mehr Urlaub. Für eine glückliche Minderheit wurde die Welt zu einem gigantischen Spielplatz. Für die meisten aber gab es höchstens kurze Erholungspausen von Not und Elend, in denen die Hoffnung wie eine Blume in der Wüste aufblühen konnte.

Le balancier oscillait entre forces progressistes et réactionnaires. La première Miss Amérique noire fut élue en septembre 1983. Un an plus tard, Margie Velma Barfield devint la première femme à être exécutée aux États-Unis depuis 22 ans. Le crack fit son apparition. Ben et Jerry devinrent millionnaires en vendant des glaces. Impliqués dans des scandales, deux des pasteurs les plus populaires de la télévision américaine, Jimmy Swaggart (« péché moral ») et Jim Bakker (fraude) disparurent des écrans.

Ailleurs dans le monde, on prouva que le Linceul de Turin avait été créé de toutes pièces au Moyen Âge et que les *Journaux de Hitler* n'étaient que le produit d'une imagination fertile qui n'était pas celle du Führer. Le matador Francisco Riviera décéda de sa blessure à la cuisse et la mère du taureau criminel fut aussitôt abattue. En Angleterre, l'éventreur du Yorkshire fut inculpé du meurtre de treize femmes.

Plus de gens se mariaient et plus de gens divorçaient. Il y avait aussi plus de vacances. Pour la minorité des gens fortunés, le monde était devenu un immense terrain de jeux. Pour la majorité des gens, il y avait de brefs moments de répit, loin de la misère et du besoin, quand l'espoir fleurissait comme une fleur dans le désert.

On 29 April 1988,
the top of this
Boeing 737 was
torn off 20,000 feet
above Hawaii.
It landed safely
and only one
passenger died.

Am 29. April 1988
wurde das Dach
dieser Boeing 737 in
einer Höhe von
6000 Metern über
Hawaii fortgerissen.
Dem Piloten gelang
es, die Maschine
sicher zu landen,
lediglich ein Passa-
gier kam ums Leben.

Le 29 avril 1988, la
partie supérieure
d'un Boeing 737 fut
arrachée à 6000
mètres d'altitude
au-dessus de Hawaï.
Le pilote réussit à
atterrir et l'accident
ne fit qu'une seule
victime.

(Above) The doomed crew of the fatally flawed *Challenger* space mission, 11 November 1985. Nine weeks later all died when *Challenger* exploded after take-off (left).

(Oben) Die Unglücksbesatzung der in der Katastrophe endenden *Challenger*-Mission, 11. November 1985. Neun Wochen später starben alle Besatzungsmitglieder, als das Raumfahrzeug unmittelbar nach dem Start explodierte (links).

(Ci-dessus) L'équipage au destin tragique de *Challenger*, la navette spatiale défectueuse, 11 novembre 1985. Neuf semaines plus tard, ils furent tous tués dans l'explosion qui survint après le décollage de *Challenger* (à gauche).

A penitent atones
for sins committed
during Lent,
the Philippines,
April 1981. Such
voluntary acts of
public shame have
now become tourist
attractions.

Eine Reumütige
leistet Abbitte für
die Sünden, die sie
während der Fasten-
zeit beging, Philip-
pinen, April 1981.
Derartige öffentliche
Bekundungen der
Scham sind zu
Touristenattraktio-
nen geworden.

Une pénitente
expie ses péchés
commis pendant le
Carême, Philippines,
avril 1981. Ces
actes volontaires
d'expiation publique
sont devenus de
réelles attractions
touristiques.

JOSE MELCHER ALCANTARA/BLACK STAR/COLORIFIC!

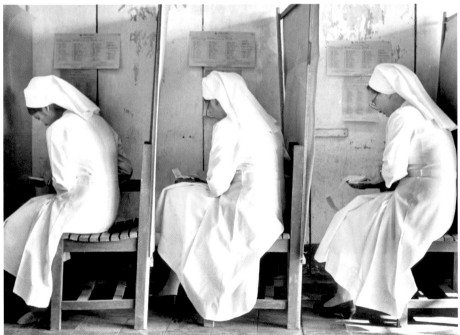

Nuns registering their votes in the presidential contest between
Ferdinand Marcos and Corazon Aquino, widow of the former
Opposition leader, the Philippines, 7 February 1986.

Nonnen bei der Stimmabgabe während der Wahl des philippinischen
Staatspräsidenten, bei der Corazon Aquino, die Witwe des früheren
Oppositionsführers, gegen Ferdinand Marcos antrat, 7. Februar 1986.

Nonnes au parloir lors de l'élection présidentielle qui opposa
Ferdinand Marcos à Corazon Aquino, la veuve de l'ancien leader
de l'opposition, Philippines, 7 février 1986.

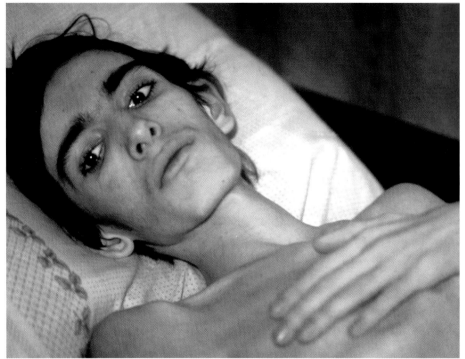

IGOR COSTIN/STERN/BLACK STAR/COLORIFIC!

One of the tens of thousands of victims of the Chernobyl disaster, Ukraine,
26 April 1986. An unauthorised test by engineers caused an explosion that started
a horrendous fire in the nuclear plant.

Ein Opfer von mehreren Zehntausend. Die Katastrophe von Tschernobyl,
Ukraine, ereignete sich, als am 26. April 1986 Ingenieure einen nicht genehmigten
Test durchführten. Es kam zu einer Explosion, die einen Großbrand in dem
Atomkraftwerk auslöste.

Une des dizaines de milliers de victimes de la catastrophe de Tchnernobyl,
Ukraine, 26 avril 1986. Une explosion causée par un essai non-autorisé effectué
par des ingénieurs causa un terrible incendie dans la centrale nucléaire.

A relation holds a photograph of one of more than 2,500 people killed when toxic gas leaked from the Union Carbide plant in Bhopal, India, 13 December 1984. It was only one of a series of leaks. Union Carbide later paid out $470 million in compensation.

Eine Verwandte zeigt das Bild von einem der mehr als 2500 Opfer, die starben, als Giftgase aus der Union-Carbide-Fabrik im indischen Bhopal austraten, 13. Dezember 1984. Es war nur ein Leck unter vielen. Später zahlte Union Carbide 470 Millionen US-Dollar Entschädigung.

Une mère avec la photographie de l'une des 2500 victimes de la pollution causée par l'émanation de gaz toxiques hors de l'usine de Union Carbide à Bhopal, Inde, 13 décembre 1984. Union Carbide versa par la suite 470 millions de dollars à titre de dédommagements.

CEM AKKAN/ANZENBERGER/COLORIFIC!

Whirling dervishes perform their traditional trance-inducing dance at the House of Mevlevi, Istanbul, Turkey. The dancers spin round sixty times a minute for periods of up to half an hour.

Wirbelnde Derwische vollführen ihren traditionellen, Trancezustände hervorrufenden Tanz, Haus des Mevlevi, Istanbul, Türkei. Bis zu einer halben Stunde drehen sich die Männer mit einer Geschwindigkeit von 60 Umdrehungen pro Minute um die eigene Achse.

Des dervishes tourbillonnants accomplissent leur danse qui les met en transe à la Maison de Mevlevi, Istanbul, Turquie. Les danseurs effectuent soixante tours à la minute et peuvent maintenir ce rythme pendant une demi-heure.

FAUSTO GIACCONE/ANZENBERGER/COLORIFIC!

Mennonites on the march in Paraguay in the 1980s. Many Anabaptist followers in the footsteps of their 16th-century founder Menno Simons left Europe for South America in the 1950s, and established religious colonies in Paraguay.

Mennoniten unterwegs, Paraguay, achtziger Jahre. Viele Anhänger des im 16. Jahrhundert lebenden Wiedertäufers Menno Simons wanderten in den fünfziger Jahren aus Europa nach Südamerika aus und gründeten in Paraguay religiöse Gemeinschaften.

Mennonites à pied au Paraguay dans les années 1980. Beaucoup d'anabaptistes sur les traces de Menno Simmons, fondateur de ce courant au 16ᵉ siècle, quittèrent l'Europe pour l'Amérique latine dans les années 1950 et établirent des colonies religieuses au Paraguay.

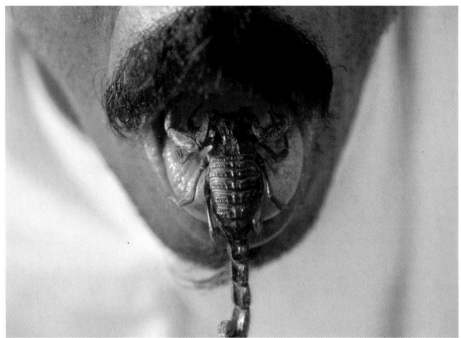

At one with nature… A scorpion worshipper admits the object of
his reverence to the temple of his mouth, Morocco. No one should
doubt that considerable faith is involved here.

Einssein mit der Natur … Ein Skorpion-Verehrer lässt das Objekt
seines Kultes in seinen Mund kriechen, Marokko. Da gehört
zweifellos Glaube dazu.

En osmose avec la nature … Un adorateur de scorpion autorise
l'objet de son culte à pénétrer dans le temple de sa bouche, Maroc.
Tout le monde conviendra aisément que cet homme fait preuve
d'une foi inébranlable.

At more than one
with nature…
A contestant in the
1985 Bee Beard
Competition. Let's
hope he was the
winner.

Weitere Steigerung:
menschlicher
Bienenstock bei
einem Wettbewerb,
1985. Ob er wohl
gewonnen hat?

En osmose totale
avec la nature …
Un participant au
concours de barbe
d'abeilles en 1985.
Espérons pour lui
qu'il remporta le
tournoi.

RICHARD HOWARD/BLACK STAR/COLORIFIC!

A pair of mice used in genetic research at the Jackson Laboratory, Maine, 1983. Laboratories that used rodents were usually safe from animal rights activists. Those that used cats or dogs, or anything larger, weren't.

Ein für die Genforschung eingesetztes Mäusepaar im Jackson Laboratory, Maine, 1983. Forschungs-labors, die mit den Nagern experimentierten, waren in aller Regel sicher vor Tierschutzaktivisten. Für Einrichtungen, die auf Katzen, Hunde und größere Tiere zurückgriffen, galt das nicht.

Deux souris utilisées pour des recherches en génétique au laboratoire Jackson, Maine, 1983. Les laboratoires qui utilisaient des rongeurs pour leurs recherches étaient rarement la cible des militants pour les droits des animaux, contrairement aux laboratoires qui se servaient de chats et de chiens.

MICHAEL MONTFORT/VISAGES/COLORIFIC!

The harpoon that cures. Fish become aquatic 'guinea pigs' as they are used for research into the properties of acupuncture. The surprising outcome would seem to be how little the needles have affected the fishes' balance.

Heilende Harpunen? Fische als aquatische Versuchskaninchen bei Forschungen zum Nutzen der Akupunktur. Überraschend, dass die Nadeln den Gleichgewichtssinn der Fische kaum stören.

Le harpon qui soigne. Les poissons devinrent les cobayes de recherches menées sur les propriétés de l'acupuncture. Aussi étonnant que cela puisse paraître, il semblerait que les aiguilles aient très peu affecté l'équilibre des poissons.

CHARLES MASON/BLACK STAR/COLORIFIC!

One of a series of photographs recording the harvesting of reindeer antlers in Alaska, 1989. By the late 1980s the antlers had become more valuable than the meat, providing much-needed income to a remote state of the USA.

Ein Bild aus einer Fotoserie über die Geweihernte in Alaska, 1989. In den späten achtziger Jahren waren die Geweihe der Rene wesentlich wertvoller als ihr Fleisch. Das begehrte Gut brachte dringend benötigte Verdienstmöglichkeiten für den entlegensten Bundesstaat der USA.

Cliché d'un reportage consacré à la « récolte » de bois de rennes en Alaska, 1989. Vers la fin des années 1980, les bois valaient plus cher que la viande, offrant ainsi une source de revenus très appréciable pour cet État américain, éloigné de tout.

A young warrior from one of Africa's smallest tribes prepares to deliver the *coup de grâce* to a hippopotamus, Lake Turkana, Kenya. The tribe, who both worshipped and hunted hippos, numbered only thirty-seven in the 1980s.

Ein junger Krieger eines der kleinsten Stämme Afrikas gibt einem Flusspferd den Gnadenstoß, Turkanasee, Kenia. Der Stamm, der Flusspferde verehrte und zugleich jagte, umfasste in den achtziger Jahren nicht mehr als 37 Menschen.

Un jeune guerrier d'une des plus petites tribus d'Afrique se prépare à porter le coup de grâce à cet hippopotame, Lac Turkana, Kenya. La tribu, qui vénérait les hippopotames autant qu'elle les chassait, ne comptait plus que 37 membres dans les années 1980.

CLAUDE CHARLIER/BLACK STAR/COLORIFIC!

Putting it on… A contestant in the *Guinness Book of Records* World's Heaviest Man Contest, Japan, April 1986. To beat the all-time record, held by Robert Earl Hughes, the contestant had to weigh in at over 485 kilograms.

Und immer noch ein Pfund drauf … Teilnehmer eines Guinness-Buch-Wettbewerbs um den Titel des schwersten Manns der Erde, Japan, April 1986. Wer den Weltrekord erringen wollte, musste mehr auf die Waage bringen als Rekordhalter Robert Earl Hughes (485 Kilogramm).

Grossir … Un participant au concours de l'homme le plus lourd du monde organisé par le Guinness Book of Records, Japon, avril 1986. Pour battre le record de tous les temps, détenu par Robert Earl Hughes, le concurrent devait peser au moins 485 kg.

Taking it off… Two aspiring weight losers appear to be in good heart (they'd need to be) at this Diet Disco in the Landmark Hotel, Durham, North Carolina, May 1989. Obesity was reaching epidemic proportions in the Unites States.

Und Pfunde runter … Zwei Aspiranten beim Abspecken in der Diätdisco, Landmark Hotel, Durham, North Carolina, Mai 1989. Übergewicht wurde in den Vereinigten Staaten zur Volkskrankheit.

Maigrir … Ces deux « apprentis-minceur » rient de bon cœur (qu'il valait mieux avoir solide) à la soirée Disco Régime organisée au Landmark Hotel, Durham, Caroline du Nord, mai 1989. L'obésité prenait des proportions épidémiques aux États-Unis.

Bronze beauty.
Catherine Wilke
(standing) passes
shelves of sun-
bathers on the
Mediterranean
island of Capri,
August 1980.

Beauty in Bronze.
Catherine Wilke
(stehend) vor gesta-
pelten Sonnen-
anbeterinnen auf
der Mittelmeerinsel
Capri, August 1980.

Beauté de bronze.
Catherine Wilke
(debout) devant une
superposition de
femmes prenant un
bain de soleil sur l'île
de Capri en Médi-
terranée, août 1980.

Golden greed.
Fortune hunters
digging for gold in
the province of Para,
Brazil, 1985.

Goldrausch.
Glücksjäger bei
der Suche nach
dem Edelmetall in
der brasilianischen
Provinz Para, 1985.

Soif d'or. Des chas-
seurs de fortune
creusent pour
trouver de l'or
dans la province de
Para, Brésil, 1985.

CLAUS MEYER/BLACK STAR/COLORIFIC!

MANFRED HORVATH/ANZENBERGER/COLORIFIC!

Hungarians, with maybe one or two Czech mates, play chess
by the pool at the Szechenyi-Bad spa, Budapest. It was the
Indian summer of Communist control in Eastern Europe.

Ungarn beim Schachspiel im Schwimmbecken eines Ferien-
hotels im Szechenyi-Bad, Budapest. Es war der letzte Sommer
der kommunistischen Herrschaft in Osteuropa.

Des Hongrois jouent aux échecs dans la piscine des bains
de Szechenyi-Bad, Budapest. Ce fut l'été indien du régime
communiste en Europe de l'Est.

Two truckers take a break from the road and concentrate on the video game consoles at Truckworld, Ohio. Hopefully, the machines make it quite clear exactly where the coin is to be inserted to start the machine.

Zwei Lastwagenfahrer machen Pause und hocken gebannt vor dem Spielautomaten in Truckworld, Ohio. Hoffentlich bleibt kein Zweifel, in welchen Schlitz die Münze geschoben werden muss, um das Spiel zu beginnen.

Détente pour deux chauffeurs de camion qui, après la route, concentrent leur attention sur ces jeux vidéo à Truckworld, Ohio. Espérons que les machines indiquent exactement où insérer la monnaie pour commencer le jeu.

The big match, US-style… Safety helmets at rakish angles, teams compete in a game of motorised croquet, Black Rock Desert, near Gerlach, Nevada, 1987. The setting is ideal for the game – a level surface, plenty of space and no rain.

Ballspiel, US-Stil … Mit Sicherheitshelmen bewaffnete Mannschaften spielen Motor-Crocket in der Nähe von Gerlach, Nevada, 1987. Der Spielort ist ideal: ebener Boden, viel Platz, kein Regen.

Le grand match, à l'américaine … Casques de sécurité sur la tête, les équipes se livrent à une partie de croquet motorisé dans le désert de Black Rock, près de Gerlach, Nevada, 1987. Le lieu est idéal pour ce jeu, le terrain est plat, l'espace ne manque pas et il ne pleut pas.

The big match, Indian-style… Nellie the Striker (newly transferred from Madras United for a record fee of three rupees per pound) bears down on goal in a game of elephant football. Why doesn't the goalie nip out and whip the ball away from her tusks?

Ballspiel, indischer Stil … Stürmerin Nellie (jüngst von Madras United für eine Rekordablöse-summe von drei Rupien pro Pfund verkauft) auf dem Weg zum Tor beim Elefantenfußball. Warum nur kommt der Tormann nicht heraus, um ihr den Ball von den Stoßzähnen fortzuschlagen?

Le grand match, à l'indienne … Nellie la butteuse (récemment transférée de Madras United pour un montant record de six roupies par kilo) charge en direction des buts au cours d'un match de football pour éléphants. Pourquoi est-ce que le gardien de but ne s'avance pas et dégage la balle de ses défenses … ?

Index

gettyimages

Over 70 million images and 30,000 hours of film footage are held by the various collections owned by Getty Images. These cover a vast number of subjects from the earliest photojournalism to current press photography, sports, social history and geography. Getty Images' conceptual imagery is renowned amongst creative end users.

www.gettyimages.com

Über 70 Millionen Bilder und 30 000 Stunden Film befinden sich in den verschiedenen Archiven von Getty Images. Sie decken ein breites Spektrum an Themen ab – von den ersten Tagen des Fotojournalismus bis hin zu aktueller Pressefotografie, Sport, Sozialgeschichte und Geographie. Bei kreativen Anwendern ist das Material von Getty Images für seine ausdrucksstarke Bildsprache bekannt.

www.gettyimages.com

Plus de 70 millions d'images et 30 000 heures de films sont détenus par les différentes collections dont Getty Images est le propriétaire. Cela couvre un nombre considérable de sujets – des débuts du photojournalisme aux photographies actuelles de presse, de sport, d'histoire sociale et de géographie. Le concept photographique de Getty Images est reconnu des créatifs.

www.gettyimages.com

Acknowledgements

The picture editor is grateful to the following individuals and agencies or collections with which they are associated for their assistance with this book:

Christopher Angeloglou, Julius Domoney, David Leverton and Sally Ryall (Colorific!); Anh Stack and Michelle Hernandez (Black Star); Rosa Di Salvo, Richard Ellis, Bob Hechler, Hilary Johnston, Robert Pepper, Eric Smalkin (Liaison Agency); Rob Harborne, Lee Martin and Matthew Stevens (Allsport); Mitch Blank, Kathy Lavelle, Eric Rachlis, Peter Rohowsky and Arlete Santos (Hulton|Archive, New York); Antonia Hille, Sarah Kemp and Alex Linghorn (Hulton|Archive, London); Jake Cunningham (PYMCA); Martin Stephens and Milica Timotic (PA News); Gul Duzyol and Jocelyne Manfredi (Sipa Press); Judith Caul and Tony Mancini (*The Guardian*); Jim Docherty and Marianne Lassen (S.I.N.); Simon Kenton (Idols); and to Sara Green and Stephanie Hudson for their kind assistance in New York and London respectively.